Cambridge Elements

Elements in Pragmatics

edited by
Jonathan Culpeper
Lancaster University, UK
Michael Haugh
University of Queensland, Australia

PRAGMATICS IN THE HEALTH SCIENCES

Maria Garraffa
University of East Anglia

Greta Mazzaggio
University of Florence

Shaftesbury Road, Cambridge CB2 8EA, United Kingdom

One Liberty Plaza, 20th Floor, New York, NY 10006, USA

477 Williamstown Road, Port Melbourne, VIC 3207, Australia

314–321, 3rd Floor, Plot 3, Splendor Forum, Jasola District Centre,
New Delhi – 110025, India

103 Penang Road, #05–06/07, Visioncrest Commercial, Singapore 238467

Cambridge University Press is part of Cambridge University Press & Assessment,
a department of the University of Cambridge.

We share the University's mission to contribute to society through the pursuit
of education, learning and research at the highest international levels of excellence.

www.cambridge.org
Information on this title: www.cambridge.org/9781009496001

DOI: 10.1017/9781009496018

First published 2025

A catalogue record for this publication is available from the British Library

ISBN 978-1-009-49600-1 Hardback
ISBN 978-1-009-49602-5 Paperback
ISSN 2633-6464 (online)
ISSN 2633-6456 (print)

Additional resources for this publication at www.cambridge.org/Garraffa

Pragmatics in the Health Sciences

Elements in Pragmatics

DOI: 10.1017/9781009496018
First published online: January 2025

Maria Garraffa
University of East Anglia

Greta Mazzaggio
University of Florence

Author for correspondence: Maria Garraffa, m.garraffa@uea.ac.uk

Abstract: This Element aims to address a gap in the literature at the intersection of linguistics, particularly pragmatics, and health sciences, such as speech and language pathology. The first section introduces the application of pragmatics concepts in healthcare and neuroscience. Section 2 discusses the development of pragmatic abilities in childhood, focusing on pragmatic communication disorder. Section 3 reviews studies on pragmatic abilities in adolescents, adults, and clinical populations, including assessments of pragmatic skills in ageing. Section 4 broadens the scope by exploring pragmatic impairments in new populations. The final section reflects on the importance of pragmatics in healthcare practice, introducing studies on mental health and intercultural pragmatics. Each section proposes discussion points to contextualise the research within debates on health pragmatics. The Element also includes a glossary (available as online supplementary material) to assist interdisciplinary audiences in understanding clinical pragmatics terminology.

Keywords: experimental pragmatics, linguistics, pragmatics, clinical linguistics, neuropragmatics.

ISBNs: 9781009496001 (HB), 9781009496025 (PB), 9781009496018 (OC)
ISSNs: 2633-6464 (online), 2633-6456 (print)

Contents

1 Why Pragmatics in Health Sciences

Research into pragmatic communication disorders has expanded the scope of investigation. Studies have examined pragmatic impairments across varied clinical profiles throughout development. This has led to a more encompassing understanding of the diverse behaviours implicated beyond conventional speech acts and conversational skills to include complex abilities such as narrative competence and comprehension of non-literal language. A broader conceptualisation has allowed for greater variability in presentations across populations. Deficits stem from an interplay of linguistic, cognitive, and social factors, complicating definitive characterisations. An isolated focus on brain regions is inadequate – a network-based neurocognitive framework is needed to delineate implicated circuits and regions underlying pragmatic functions. Additionally, evidence points to a distributed neural model rather than localisation. This Element aims to integrate findings from clinical pragmatics, experimental pragmatics, and theoretical pragmatics. It provides an overview of evolving issues from diversifying clinical profiles assessed as well as the range of behaviours and neuropragmatics investigations undertaken. Unifying these domains may further the comprehension of the heterogeneous nature and multifaceted mechanisms underlying pragmatic communication in both clinical and non-clinical settings.

1.1 What Is Clinical Pragmatics

Pragmatics is a branch of linguistics concerned with how language is used in context to convey meaning. The term 'pragmatic language ability' within this context refers to the skill to use language appropriately within various social and situational contexts. This includes a distinction drawn between linguistic-pragmatics and social-pragmatics (a.o., Andrés-Roqueta & Katsos, 2020). Linguistic-pragmatics primarily involves understanding and using language in ways that conform to grammatical rules and semantic conventions. It focuses on the pragmatic use of language within its structural framework, such as interpreting scalar inferences and conventions in language use that do not necessarily require deep **Theory of Mind** (ToM), the ability to infer mental states, intentions, and emotions of others (a concept that we will address multiple time in this Element). In contrast, social-pragmatics goes beyond linguistic structure to encompass the ability to understand and interpret communicative intentions in social interactions. It requires not only linguistic competence but also ToM. Social-pragmatics tasks involve interpreting non-literal language use, such as irony, sarcasm, and indirect speech acts, where understanding the intended meaning often involves considering the speaker's beliefs and intentions

(Andrés-Roqueta & Katsos, 2020). In this Element, we adopt a framework of pragmatics consistent with prevailing definitions in clinical and experimental research, addressing topics pertinent to these fields of study[1].

The study of pragmatic abilities in clinical populations has been fundamental in establishing clinical pragmatics as a field (see Cummings, 2017, 2021 for an overview). Clinical pragmatics is the investigation of the pragmatic processes involved in implicit and intended language, emerging at the intersection of various research areas, including linguistics, cognitive science, and sociolinguistics. Informed by theoretical pragmatics, clinical pragmatics offers a framework for more effectively assessing and designing intervention protocols for pragmatic language disorders. Conversely, it serves as a testing ground for refining theoretical models of pragmatics.

Traditionally, clinical pragmatics focused on populations directly linked to pragmatic disorders, such as autism spectrum disorder (ASD). However, recent developments have broadened its scope into several aspects of the health sciences, with studies encompassing a wider range of pragmatic phenomena, methodologies, and approaches. The need to assess pragmatic skills has revealed that this aspect of language holds relevance for several other populations beyond those traditionally associated with language disorders, such as individuals with right-hemisphere damage or traumatic brain injury (TBI) or people with addictions. Neurological conditions previously not considered to have core symptoms of language disorders have been investigated, revealing impairments in pragmatic abilities among patients with Parkinson's disease (Montemurro et al., 2019), amyotrophic lateral sclerosis (Bambini et al., 2020a), multiple sclerosis (Carotenuto et al., 2018a), as well as psychiatric conditions such as schizophrenia (Colle et al., 2013).

Terms rooted in theoretical pragmatics are increasingly applied in researching clinical populations with pragmatic disorders, often within a pragmatic conceptual framework. Concepts like **verbosity** or inability to maintain a topic are now described in terms of narrative abilities, such as the ability to navigate both micro and macro narrative structures (see Marini et al., 2008 for a study on the application of narrative analyses in schizophrenia). Researchers

---

[1] The definition we propose draws upon earlier distinctions, such as those by Leech (1983) and Thomas (1983), which differentiate between 'pragmalinguistics' and 'sociopragmatics'. Pragmalinguistics refers to the linguistic resources available for performing speech acts and conveying meaning, such as syntactic structures and semantic conventions, while sociopragmatics focuses on how these resources are applied within specific social contexts, shaped by cultural norms and expectations. However, in recent years – especially in the field of experimental pragmatics – the focus of this distinction has been on separating pragmatic phenomena that can be explained with a greater emphasis on linguistic aspects (such as syntax and semantics) from those phenomena where cognitive factors, like mental state reasoning, play a more significant role in understanding communicative intentions.

in clinical pragmatics are increasingly drawing on pragmatic theories to characterise and differentiate developmental and acquired pragmatic disorders in both children and adults. Moreover, empirical findings are expanding pragmatic theories and supporting clinical practice. Recent investigations in clinical populations have expanded beyond traditional speech acts to include examinations of narrative abilities and the comprehension of non-literal meanings in **metaphors** and irony. These studies reveal a more intricate field with deficits observed in clinical groups not traditionally investigated, such as individuals with addiction, as discussed in Section 4 of this Element.

As Cummings suggested (Cummings, 2009), clinical pragmatics is best understood as a multidisciplinary field that converges theories and evidence from multiple populations, integrating aspects from linguistics, social cognition, and cultural influences. Concerning social cognition, which involves cognitive processes in social interactions, two core factors are crucial in the study of pragmatics in the health sciences: emotion recognition and Theory of Mind. Emotion recognition is now typically assessed across different modalities, including understanding gestures in non-verbal language. Theory of Mind, as previously mentioned, refers to recognising that others have thoughts that can differ from one's own, and understanding how others' thoughts influence behaviour (Wimmer & Perner, 1983).

In this Element we would like to integrate clinical pragmatics with a broader landscape of pragmatics for the health sciences, by discussing more aspects where a contact between pragmatics and the health domain can be beneficials. For example, clinical psychologist Cavell (1990) proposed a hierarchical model of social function, emphasising the importance of positive social functioning for health. This model specifies relations among social skills, social performance, social competence, and non-social factors such as income, appearance, physical ability, motivation, and opportunity. Assessment of pragmatic communication skills should encompass these components, reflecting the focus of intervention in clinical pragmatics in a setting beyond the academics' labs.

It is noteworthy that Cavell's model shares many components with the World Health Organization International Classification of Functioning, Disability, and Health (2007), applicable to both neurorehabilitation and intervention for individuals with cognitive disorders. The **ICF framework** (Figure 1) presents three domains to characterise health outcomes: body functions and structures (including psychological functions), performance of daily activities, and participation in life situations.

Personal and environmental factors influencing outcomes, as in Cavell's 'social factors', are incorporated in the ICF framework. Both frameworks stress the importance of considering the ability to participate in meaningful social

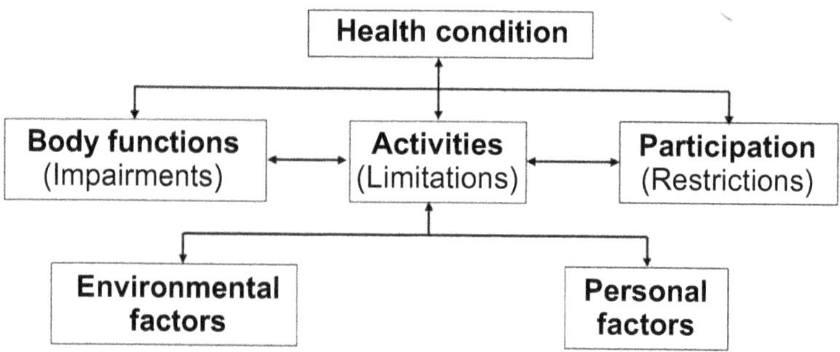

Figure 1 Framework of functioning, disability, and health (ICF)

roles and overall social competence in pragmatic communication intervention. These perspectives, as elaborated in Section 5, bear significant relevance to the contemporary healthcare system, which prioritises patient-centred outcomes and goal-setting tailored to evolving global demographics.

The challenge now lies in effectively integrating pragmatics into a healthcare model. A significant step in this direction, at least in the child population, was the recent inclusion of social (pragmatic) communication disorder (SPCD) in the **Diagnostic and Statistical Manual of Mental Disorders** (DSM-5, American Psychological Association – APA 2022), highlighting the need to incorporate pragmatics into medical practice. Additionally, there is a need to expand testing for pragmatic disorders in under-investigated groups that can be at risk and explore pragmatic domains in clinical populations further.

1.2 The Social Pragmatic Communication Disorder: Language or Cognition?

Although the diagnosis of social (pragmatic) communication disorder (SPCD) is a recent addition to the *DSM-5*, the specific exploration of pragmatic communication is entrenched in a broad discourse that shapes our present comprehension and evaluation of these crucial skills across diverse clinical populations. The fifth edition of the *Diagnostic and Statistical Manual of Mental Disorders* (DSM-5; APA, 2022) introduced SPCD as a novel diagnostic category within **neurodevelopmental disorders**, specifically within the section on communication disorders. SPCD is characterised by difficulties in utilising language for social purposes, adapting communication to context, adhering to conversational norms, and grasping implicit meanings, in absence of typical symptoms of autism. At its essence, SPCD revolves around the pragmatic ability, traditionally defined as the proficiency to employ language suitably within various contexts. More recently, this definition has broadened to encompass a multimodal perspective of communication, incorporating diverse communication tools such as non-verbal cues, alongside extralinguistic factors like facial expressions and paralinguistic features, e.g., **prosody** and tone of voice (Holler & Levinson, 2019).

While this expansion of communicative modalities is advantageous and mirrors the contemporary communication landscape, it presents a challenge for researchers and clinicians in distinguishing pragmatic communication disorders stemming from social cognition issues from those originating from impairments in other cognitive functions. For instance, an instance of over-informativeness in pragmatic communication, such as excessively divulging personal details, could indicate a deficit in Theory of Mind. Alternatively, this behaviour might stem from disinhibition and reduced self-monitoring (associated with **executive functioning** problems), constituting a distinct cognitive function and not in relation to the ToM. Moreover, it could result from an inability to interpret facial expressions (impaired emotion recognition), lack of attention to feedback (poor attentional control), or inadequate understanding of appropriate language use in varying social contexts (a semantic/cultural issue).

Identifying the specific neuropsychological facets of pragmatic communication disorders has posed a significant challenge for researchers over the past three decades. Future research on social cognition within rehabilitation populations, along with consideration of environmental factors (e.g., increasing numbers of multilingual speakers and mobility), is likely to enhance our comprehension of pragmatics.

Irrespective of the expressive aspect of SPCD, pragmatics denotes the ability to bridge the substantial gap between the literal and intended meaning of a communicative act. Numerous tools in pragmatics have been proposed to explore intentions in conversations, such as indirect speech acts, irony, metaphors, and other forms of figurative language. Typically, the ability to detect pragmatic patterns in both production and comprehension during conversations follows a predetermined developmental trajectory, as outlined in Section 2, with a series of expected pragmatic abilities emerging by preschool age, heavily influenced by a child's environment. The study of developmental pragmatics has been pivotal in investigating neurodevelopmental disorders such as autism spectrum disorder (ASD). However, the focus on pragmatic impairments in ASD has sometimes overshadowed research into other neurodevelopmental disorders, such as developmental language disorders (DLD) and attention deficit hyperactivity disorder (ADHD) (Bishop, 2014; Green et al., 2014).

Given that pragmatics encompasses a diverse array of abilities, investigations in this domain can be approached from various perspectives, leading to inevitable issues with inconsistent terminology (see Gabbatore et al., 2023 for an overview). SPCD has been conceptualised as both a syndrome and a disorder, with its core symptoms situated within the realm of social communication disorder, overlapping with ASD, a distinct neurodevelopmental syndrome. It is imperative to investigate, within a finer framework, which aspects of social communication are impaired, utilising clear tools from pragmatics, Theory of Mind, and social communication. Pragmatic difficulties have also been considered a **comorbidity** factor in ADHD, necessitating further research to elucidate the core language-based pragmatic deficit and its relationship with impulsive and hyperactive behaviour in this population.

The lack of a differential diagnosis for SPCD, which may exhibit very similar symptoms to populations with DLD, ADHD, and ASD, underscores the need for clearer results in comparative studies both within and across syndromes. In the development of future clinical tools for pragmatics, it is recommended to consider various aspects of pragmatic communication, incorporating elements from a range of cognitive abilities and examining the interplay between pragmatic abilities and **executive functions**, as well as Theory of Mind. Additionally, as discussed in Section 5, cultural and linguistic backgrounds are essential components, yet currently, no defined guidelines exist for constructing a comprehensive pragmatic assessment.

Lastly, for a more robust investigation of SPCD across syndromes, it is essential to incorporate not only linguistics-based phenomena but also extralinguistic factors and multimodalities, which are integral to contemporary communication. These factors could play a pivotal role, for example, in distinguishing the source of SPCD between ADHD and more language-based syndromes.

1.3 Evidence for a Pragmatic Brain

Traditionally, pragmatics was studied through approaches within linguistics grounded in theoretical models and based on data from transcribed language interactions. However, from the 1980s, the field began adopting quantitative, empirically rigorous methods from cognitive psychology and neuroscience. This interdisciplinary approach aimed to unveil the cognitive underpinnings of pragmatic phenomena through controlled experiments. The field of neuropragmatics emerged after approximately two decades of studies on pragmatic difficulties in clinical populations and rapidly incorporated methods and inquiries from cognitive neuroscience, such as neuroimaging and physiological measures (Bischetti et al., 2024). The neuroimaging literature on pragmatics has extensively explored text and discourse processing, revealing evidence for the involvement of extended brain circuits from both hemispheres in processing pragmatic meanings at the level of larger language units. These bilateral effects support the notion that a clear lateralisation of pragmatic knowledge, for example in the right hemisphere, does not fully represent the operations involved in the pragmatic brain. Bilateral effects in frontotemporal or fronto-parietal regions have been reported, for instance, for establishing coherence in text comprehension (Ferstl & von Cramon, 2001) and inference processes in logical connectives (Prado et al., 2015).

One well-investigated pragmatic aspect in neuroimaging literature is the comprehension of metaphorical expressions. Studies compare the process during the comprehension of a metaphor with a literal meaning expressed in word pairs. For example, by comparing the processing of an expression such as '*It takes a village to raise a child*' and its literal meaning '*Children's education requires many resources*'. Research has shown greater activations for metaphorical vs. literal items in language areas in both hemispheres, often paired with activations of regions related to executive functions, such as the anterior cingulate cortex bilaterally (e.g., Bambini et al., 2011). One speculation could be the involvement of an inhibitory control process for irrelevant information in the literal meaning expression. However, brain activation during metaphorical comprehension also involves the Theory of Mind brain circuits (see Siegal & Varlery, 2002 for a review of ToM neural systems) indicating additional processing related to mutual comprehension in inferring the intended meaning conveyed via metaphors.

Another phenomenon investigated in neuroimaging studies is verbal humour, with studies reporting an involvement of frontotemporal language-related areas (Goel & Dolan, 2001; Vrticka et al., 2013)), as well as regions involved in reasoning about others and core aspects of processing conflicting information.

Recently, pragmatics intervention (see Parson et al., 2017 for an overview on different pragmatics intervention techniques) has been proposed for several populations, including clinical ones, but also for non-pathological ageing (Bambini et al., 2020b). The training programme, discussed in Section 3, recorded an increase in pragmatic abilities in the subjects across several domains, including metaphor comprehension and sustained topics.

This neurologically based approach to the effects of pragmatic abilities is promising, but more research is needed to explore how to optimise social communication across different populations and throughout the lifespan.

1.4 Experimental Pragmatics: Testing Our Mutual Understanding

Conveying pragmatic meaning involves a specific inferential process applied to every linguistic act, differing notably from literal expressions, particularly when embedded in metaphorical or ironic contexts.

Pioneering work by Noveck and Sperber (Noveck, 2001; Noveck & Sperber, 2004) has formalised this intricate line of inquiry into the inferential process required for pragmatic meaning under the designation of 'Experimental Pragmatics'. Unlike purely theoretical descriptions, experimental pragmatics seeks to explore the cognitive and neural mechanisms underlying our comprehension and production of context-dependent meanings. By precisely quantifying pragmatic behaviours and the underlying processing involved, it establishes a direct link between pragmatic competence and the cognitive resources necessary for this competence.

For instance, empirical studies among adults have shown that refined pragmatic competence is associated with a processing cost, as observed in the comprehension of under-informative statements like 'Some dogs are mammals' compared to absolute statements such as 'All mammals are dogs' (Bott & Noveck, 2004). The use of 'some' can be true with a semantic ('some and perhaps all') or false with a narrowed ('some but not all') reading. Notably, responses reflecting narrowed interpretations become more frequent as response latency increases to 3 seconds. This is an example of extra processing due to a pragmatic non-felicitous statement.

However, it is essential to recognise that pragmatic meaning is not solely based on specific types of inferential processing. The experimental pragmatic agenda should not isolate this aspect of language as distinct from other processing demands, such as word retrieval in the lexicon or parsing a grammatical sentence. Pragmatic knowledge lies at the heart of communication across all contexts and necessitates adapting this process to varying conditions. Consequently, individual variation is a crucial component of experimental investigations, which must consider cognitive abilities, personal factors, and environmental circumstances. Even with these considerations, experimental pragmatics must address the significant impact that factors such as the language spoken, the task chosen, and the cultural background of the speaker can have, making it challenging to generalise research findings as universal (Kecskes, 2014).

For example, considering irony, its comprehension assumes that the interlocutor will grasp the pragmatics of the ironic utterance. However, this understanding can be influenced by the situation and may extend beyond mere language processing, sometimes involving personal perceptions of the speaker, multiple layers of associated meanings, with certain aspects possibly understood as behavioural responses in a laboratory setting. It is crucial to select the appropriate task, and further research is necessary to determine the relationship between a task and the interpretation of an ironic message, for instance, by collecting additional converging evidence to consider the emotional response across production, reading, or listening tasks.

1.5 The Structure of the Element

This Element is written with the assumption that the reader possesses a foundational understanding of pragmatics and is familiar with key terminologies in the field. However, to ensure clarity and accessibility, all linguistic terms, including those more commonly recognised, are defined in the Glossary. Recognising the diverse backgrounds of our readership, which may include multilingual speakers and experts from various disciplines, we have incorporated discussion points in lieu of traditional summaries. These points are designed to foster further investigation and dialogue at the intersection of pragmatics and health sciences. Medical terminology is restricted to the most prevalent terms used in Clinical Psychology and Speech Pathology, all of which are also defined in the Glossary.

This Element addresses the need for an updated overview of research in pragmatics within the health domain, outlining key milestones in its development across the lifespan. It lays the foundation for a deeper exploration of pragmatics' impact beyond the language sciences. By providing essential insights into the principles of pragmatics and their application in health sciences, this Element broadens the scope for researchers and equips them with the requisite knowledge to navigate this expansive field. It is particularly crafted for researchers – linguists, psychologists, or pathologists – interested in applying theoretical tools of pragmatics to anticipate global trends, such as migration and an ageing population.

In addressing pragmatics in health sciences, we also explore pragmatics in typical populations, such as its development in typically developing children and in bilinguals. This inclusion is crucial because understanding typical pragmatic development provides a comprehensive baseline against which atypical or clinical populations can be compared. Moreover, studying pragmatics in typical populations helps in identifying universal principles and variations that are essential for developing effective communication strategies in health-related contexts. By including diverse populations, we aim to present a holistic view of pragmatics, demonstrating its relevance and application across various stages of life and sociolinguistic backgrounds.

The primary objective of this Element is to explore the evolution of pragmatics over recent decades and its implications for the study of a richer set of populations not primarily associated with social pragmatic communication disorders. This opening section has provided a contextual framework for pragmatics in the health sciences within an interdisciplinary landscape, encompassing various healthcare models and recent pivotal research findings in neuroscience and experimental pragmatics.

It is imperative to acknowledge that environmental factors, particularly participation in everyday life situations, are integral components of the International Classification of Functioning, Disability, and Health (ICF) model, essential for overall health. Subsequent sections will delve into several clinical domains to reinforce the central notion that communication abilities are quantifiable and fundamental aspects of healthcare practice across a diverse array of clinical populations.

Section 2 will address the developmental stages of pragmatics in typical and atypical development, considering both the developmental timeline expected within specific age groups and the potential influences of a rich environment, such as growing up in a multilingual family.

Section 3 will examine communication abilities across the lifespan, focusing on healthy ageing. It will discuss the cognitive and social use of language in older adults, the role of pragmatics in diagnosing dementia and mild cognitive impairments, the impact of neurological events on pragmatic abilities, and the power of swearing. This section will also explore new therapeutic approaches designed to enhance pragmatic abilities in individuals who require support.

Section 4 will explore well-studied syndromes characterised by core impairments in pragmatic abilities, such as autism spectrum disorder (ASD) or attention deficit hyperactivity disorder (ADHD), alongside emerging populations where pragmatics may be atypical due to factors such as addiction or medical conditions like multiple sclerosis.

Section 5, the concluding section, will address pragmatic abilities from a healthcare perspective, tackling various issues including methods for assessing pragmatic abilities in clinical settings, the impact of non-literal expressions in patient–clinician communication, and the urgent need to expand methodologies for investigating pragmatic abilities within clinical populations. It will emphasise the importance of an integrated care system that considers both environmental and personal communication abilities.

Upon completing this Element, readers will have acquired a deep understanding of the intersection between pragmatics and health sciences, along with practical insights and applications relevant for both researchers and practitioners in these fields.

2 Pragmatic Development

In contrast to semantics, or syntax, which grows quickly in early infancy, mastering sophisticated conversational skills takes time. This section discusses pragmatic development from early childhood through the school years and adolescence. In the first years, children gain comprehension of joint attention and intentional communication through gestures before producing words. Around ages 3–5, they begin adapting messages based on the interlocutor and establishing referential agreements. School-aged children acquire implicatures and figurative language skills. Around age 6, they understand irony, while scalar implicatures pose challenges linked to lexical knowledge. Comprehension improves with age as linguistic and cognitive abilities mature. In adolescence, pragmatic competence strongly influences peer acceptance as dramatic changes occur. Recent studies shed light on the fundamental role of Theory of Mind and narrative abilities. Research also examines bilingual pragmatics and investigates how native status influences tolerance of pragmatic anomalies in non-native speech. Assessments effectively identify pragmatic impairments, though it is difficult to capture its multidimensional nature.

2.1 First Steps in Pragmatic Development: Early Years

The field of early pragmatic development first emerged in scholarly literature in the mid-1970s. Halliday (1975) was a pioneering figure in this area, as were other researchers who started analysing young children's communication through the lens of **Speech Act Theory** (a.o., Austin, 1975; Bates et al., 1975; Bruner, 1975; Searle, 1969). Over the past two decades, there has been a growing experimental interest in pragmatic development, together with the acquisition of cognitive abilities essential for expressing and recognising communicative intentions. This heightened attention is driven, in part, by the acknowledgement of its foundational role in children's language acquisition.

In the early stages of development, children's communicative repertoire consists primarily of non-verbal behaviours and prelinguistic vocalisations that differ from adult language structures. The first seeds of pragmatic development begin emerging within the first few years of a child's life, as they start to grasp some key social functions of communication. According to Stephens and Matthews (2014: 14), 'the pre-verbal stages of our lives are *pure* pragmatics' since 'we approach communication at this time without grammar or lexicon, and yet children really do seem to master the "uses" of language before they have learned to utter or comprehend a single word of it [. . .]. Indeed, recent evidence suggests that this very early pragmatic development is key in the acquisition of language proper'. The relationships between communicative acts and their social-physical context involve mastery of communicative forms as well as a growing ability to interpret situational components. Specifically, productive and receptive communication depends on both deploying a variety of signals appropriately and comprehending the multiple elements – social and environmental – that comprise any given communicative exchange.

As research on early pragmatic development has evolved, it has become clear that at the core of this process seems to be the development of socio-cognitive abilities related to **Theory of Mind**. The concept of Theory of Mind was originally introduced by Premack and Woodruff (1978) to explore whether nonhuman primates represent others' mental states and has been defined as a 'theory' because it is a system of inferences, enabling individuals to predict the behaviour of others by considering their inferred mental states. Subsequently, developmental psychologists adopted this framework to examine children's representations of their own and others' minds in both typical and atypical development. A commonly proposed view is that communication relies on interlocutors mutually representing one another's intentions, suggesting the capacity to understand others' perspectives acts as a prerequisite for communication. Additionally, scholars have suggested impaired social communication, as seen in autism, could stem from flaws in Theory of Mind development (a.o., Baron-Cohen et al., 1985). While contemporary understanding acknowledges that certain forms of communication may not necessitate a fully developed Theory of Mind, and we will explore how some pragmatic interpretations can occur without accessing the interlocutor's knowledge, it remains crucial to recognise the inherent connection between pragmatic development and various cognitive abilities, including Theory of Mind.

Given the importance of Theory of Mind in linguistic and pragmatic development, it soon became necessary to devise tests aimed at capturing the development of this ability in children. One of the most well-known tests is the 'false beliefs' test (or 'Sally and Anne' test, Baron-Cohen et al., 1985; Wimmer & Perner, 1983) which assesses whether children can inhibit their own knowledge and infer another's mistaken belief about an object's location (Figure 2). In the Sally and Anne test, participants are told a short story involving two characters: Sally and Anne (a). Sally places a ball in her basket before leaving the room for a walk (b). While Sally is away, Anne moves the ball from the basket to a box (c). When Sally returns, the child is asked where Sally will look for the ball (d). A child who has developed a Theory of Mind would predict that Sally will look in the basket, as Sally is unaware that Anne moved the ball while she was gone.

This understanding, known as false belief comprehension, typically develops between the ages of three and five years, marking an important milestone in children's cognitive and social development.

However, research shows Theory of Mind consists of various precursor skills emerging earlier and in a predictable order: for example, children typically develop an awareness that two persons can have different *desires* for the same object before they realise that two individuals can have different *beliefs* about

Figure 2 Schema of the Sally and Anne test, used to assess children's Theory of Mind. In (a), Sally and Anne are introduced. Sally has a basket, and Anne has a box. In (b), Sally places a ball in her basket and leaves. In (c), while Sally is away, Anne moves the ball to the box. Finally, in (d), Sally returns, and the participant is asked, 'Where will Sally look for the ball?' This test measures whether the child understands that Sally holds a false belief about the ball's location.

the same object. Moreover, their understanding of *diverse beliefs* tends to emerge before the comprehension of *false beliefs* (Wellman & Liu, 2004). While not constituting a fully fledged Theory of Mind, these early pragmatic precursors around the first years of life suggest socio-cognitive underpinnings of linguistic development, even prior to false belief understanding milestones. Abilities central to Theory of Mind, such as perceiving others as intentional agents and comprehending the speaker's meaning, have been shown to act as precursor capacities enabling toddlers' first demonstrations of communicative intention through gestures and words (a.o., Carpenter et al., 1998).

Engaging in joint attention involves synchronising one's focus with that of a social partner on a third object or event. Early manifestations involve responding to cues made by others through their *eye gaze* or the use of *pointing gestures* to redirect attention. Infants first display the ability to follow a partner's gaze or motions aimed at enlisting shared focus. Over time, they begin initiating such cues themselves through eye contact, looking between an object and a social partner, or using deictic gestures to actively engage others in jointly attending to something in the external environment. In the latter half of the first year of life, typically between eight and twelve months, Bates et al. (1975) proposed the emergence of the earliest deictic gestures, including showing, giving, and pointing. These initial gestures play a crucial role, marking the initiation of intentional communication, empowering the child to initiate the first triadic interactions, and establishing the groundwork for the subsequent development of symbols and language. Indeed, the pointing gestures observed in interactions between 14-month-olds and their mothers, as reported by Rowe (2000), are predominantly employed to direct the other's attention and predict future vocabulary development (Rowe et al., 2008). In sum, infants' use of gestures and the ability to engage in episodes of joint attention have long been studied as precursors to later language skills and current findings provide some support for the hypothesis that both are reflections of a similar underlying social-cognitive skill and that they do both uniquely predict later language ability (Salo et al., 2018).

As children develop, they show the ability to use pragmatic inferences to maximise communicative effectiveness. For example, two-year-olds provide more information (naming objects and performing referential gestures) to help an interlocutor find a hidden object when the interlocutor does not know where the object is hidden. Between ages three and five, there is a gradual improvement in adapting communication to the interlocutor by selecting the type of information provided depending on whether their partner knows the relevant facts and objects. Additionally, starting at age three, children begin to create temporary referential agreements during conversations, leading interlocutors to select not only the specific information to include but also which words to use based on the partner's specific expectations. For example, Matthews et al. (2010) found that by age three, children develop expectations regarding the referential expressions used by interlocutors to name an object. In their experiment, children were slower to react to commands when a familiar interlocutor named an object using a new referential expression (e.g., 'horse') compared to their usual expression (e.g., 'pony'). This did not occur with an unfamiliar interlocutor where no referential agreement had been established.

In recent years, there has been substantial empirical research exploring children's pragmatic inferences by drawing on frameworks from linguistic pragmatics, such as Grice's (1975) theory of **conversational implicatures**. Researchers have employed understandings from pragmatics to investigate how children start making inferences early in development by considering the speaker's intentions, highlighting the role of social cognition in communication. Despite this shared emphasis, Bohn and Frank (2019) highlighted the apparent contradiction between findings from research on the origins of language and the development of linguistic pragmatics. While studies depict one-year-olds as deeply attuned to communicative intentions, research on phenomena like **scalar implicatures** reveals pragmatic challenges until the age of six (Foppolo et al., 2021; further discussed in Section 2.2). To reconcile these divergent data streams, researchers have employed different approaches, one of which is the Rational Speech Act (RSA) framework. This approach relies on mathematical formalisation of conversational actors, modelling the reasoning processes that underlie pragmatic inferences. Advocates of this framework argue for developmental continuity, suggesting that the foundations for mature pragmatic inference are laid by 6–9 months. Subsequent changes are seen as the gradual refinement of linguistic knowledge and general processing abilities as children's skills develop (Bohn & Frank, 2019).

2.2 Pragmatic Development during School Years

The analysis of developmental data is essential for comprehending how pragmatic and other behaviours evolve throughout time. Through examining the onset and progression of these actions from early childhood to maturity, scientists may recognise trends, turning points, and difficulties in the developmental process. In contrast to theoretical speculations, these developmental findings offer tangible proof that assists in developing and improving pragmatic theories. In pragmatic models, researchers have frequently concentrated on competent adult behaviour; nevertheless, by extending ideas from developmental studies, these theories can more effectively account for the complexities of human interaction throughout lifespan (Noveck, 2018; for developmental literature see Matthews, 2014).

As children reach school age, typically between four and six years old, they are exposed to a myriad of new social situations and expectations, which serve as catalysts for the continued development of their pragmatic competence. To have a better understanding of the trajectory of pragmatic language development during the school-age years, researchers have carried several experimental investigations. This emerging area of research investigates various essential pragmatic skills, particularly how children learn to understand and utilise implicatures and figurative language, including irony and metaphors. By investigating how children negotiate and understand these non-literal meanings in the framework of their developing social skills, scientists hope to shed light on the mechanisms that underlie the development of pragmatic language abilities in school-age children.

Tests of Gricean pragmatics evaluate the understanding of conversational implicatures and cooperative principles, including *relevance* (i.e., speakers should make their contributions relevant to the ongoing conversation) and *quantity* (i.e., speakers should provide an appropriate amount of information – neither too much nor too little – to fulfil the informational needs of the conversation). Mastery of these concepts typically occurs between the ages of six and eleven. A focal point in research is the acquisition of scalar implicatures, a question that gained prominence with Noveck's groundbreaking work in 2001. Scalar implicature is a phenomenon in pragmatics where the use of a particular term or expression implies the exclusion of a more informative or stronger alternative. It occurs when a speaker chooses a weaker term from a scale of meaning, such as 'some' instead of 'all', 'few' instead of 'many', or 'might' instead of 'will'. The listener infers that the speaker could have used a stronger term if it were applicable, leading to additional meaning beyond the literal interpretation of the words used. Noveck's experiments on children's comprehension of modals and quantifiers marked the inception of experimental pragmatics as a distinct discipline. In one such experiment, children assessed sentences like 'There might be a parrot in the box' when a parrot *must* necessarily be present. The results revealed that children provided statistically more logically true responses than adults (i.e., accepting the use of the less informative term *might* instead of considering the more informative term *must*). Only with age did they gradually incorporate pragmatic reasoning. Similarly, children consistently gave logically true responses to sentences like 'Some giraffes have long necks', despite the pragmatically infelicitous nature of such statements. While logically true based on the premise 'All giraffes have long necks', these sentences are considered pragmatically infelicitous due to their under-informativeness, using a weaker scalar element (*some*) compared to stronger alternatives (*all*), given that, in reality, all giraffes rather than just some have long necks.

Children's tendency towards logical interpretations of scalar terms has led to various hypotheses about the underlying causes (relevant references are vast, see Chemla & Singh, 2014). A *lexicalist account* suggests difficulties stem from incomplete lexical knowledge of scales or challenges retrieving lexical alternatives. A *pragmatic account* attributes issues to an immature pragmatic system making children more tolerant of anomalies or less adept at recognising implicated meanings. Additionally, the *processing account* links challenges to limited cognitive resources for complex semantics. Children's proficiency with **ad hoc implicatures**, computable even by preschoolers, has been argued to support the lexicalist view. Specifically, some children may have the ability to derive pragmatic inferences but face difficulties accessing established scalar alternatives, particularly when scales require lexicalisation that takes time to develop. This could explain why younger children perform better with context-dependent ad hoc than generalised scalar implicatures, with only the latter apparently linked to Theory of Mind performances (Foppolo et al., 2021).

When examining children's comprehension of figurative language, the overall complexity of the literature's findings remains challenging to navigate (for a review see Falkum & Köder, 2020). The ability to recognise irony is one of the most sophisticated pragmatic abilities, whose developmental path has been extensively studied in experimental pragmatics and developmental psychology (see Filippova, 2014 for a review). Around age six, children begin to demonstrate an understanding of verbal irony (a.o., Harris & Pexman, 2003) even if recent studies – adopting more ecologically valid and implicit tasks – suggest an earlier sensitivity may emerge by age three (Falkum & Korder, 2020). Ackerman (1983) proposed that children interpret irony in two phases: first, they detect that the literal meaning is inappropriate, and second, they infer the speaker's social motivation for using irony. While this two-step process is similar to how adults detect implicatures by recognising a maxim violation and inferring the social motivation, the literature indicates that younger children often stop at the first Detection phase. They recognise the inappropriateness of the literal meaning but may struggle to make the subsequent inference about the speaker's intent. In contrast, adults typically integrate these steps more seamlessly due to their more advanced cognitive abilities and greater contextual knowledge. Pexman and Glenwright (2007) studied irony comprehension in children ages 6–10. Scenarios with puppets were presented, and the endings could contain either ironic statements (compliments or criticisms) or neutral control statements. Comprehension was evaluated on: (a) the speaker's belief (e.g., for an ironic 'Great drawing', determining if the speaker believes it is good or bad), (b) the speaker's attitude (assessed with a 5-point nice/mean rating scale), and (c) the speaker's intention to be ironic (assessed with a 3-point teasing/real rating scale). Results showed specific developmental trends: for ironic criticisms, understanding the speaker's beliefs emerged before understanding attitude and intention, which emerged together later. For ironic compliments, understanding beliefs and intentions emerged before attitude. The authors claim social norms and conversational expectations lead us to anticipate (literally) positive comments more; ironic criticism is used more frequently than compliments, putting the latter at an interpretive disadvantage. They also argue children's ability to understand verbal irony depends on maturing Theory of Mind (second-order belief understanding) and social learning abilities. However, according to some authors, possessing a developed Theory of Mind is seen as necessary but not sufficient for irony comprehension (Bosco & Bucciarelli, 2008). One factor that seems to play a role is the ability to distinguish irony from lies and rule out the speaker communicating an obviously false message with the intention to deceive the listener (Mazzarella & Pouscoulous, 2021).

Finally, in line with the echoic account of irony (Sperber & Wilson, 1981; Wilson & Sperber, 2012), ironic expressions are more easily understood when they echo or contrast with a preceding statement or situation. This means that the context or preceding utterance plays a crucial role in clarifying the ironic intent behind a statement. This notion is supported by research conducted by Keenan and Quigley in 1999, which found that ironic expressions that explicitly reference or echo a prior statement are more readily comprehended by listeners. When the irony directly relates to or contrasts with a preceding statement, it creates a clearer signal for the listener to recognise the intended ironic meaning. Moreover, the observation that ironic criticisms are understood earlier than ironic compliments can be explained by social norms and communication patterns. In many social contexts, irony is more commonly used for criticism or negative evaluations rather than for compliments or positive remarks. This tendency reflects broader cultural norms where irony serves as a tool for expressing dissatisfaction, scepticism, or disapproval in a socially acceptable manner. Therefore, the combination of the echoic nature of irony and its prevalence in critical rather than complimentary contexts contributes to the earlier comprehension of ironic criticisms compared to ironic compliments. This trend has been observed not only in typically developing children but also in autistic children, as demonstrated in recent research by Panzeri et al. (2022). This suggests that the differential comprehension of ironic criticisms and compliments may be a universal aspect of irony processing, transcending developmental and cognitive differences.

In conclusion, while children make considerable progress in school with many linguistic skills, certain pragmatic abilities continue to develop well into later years. For example, deriving scalar implicatures and comprehending verbal irony maturationally extend into these years. Future research would benefit from more exploration of figurative language online processing in children using innovative methods. Eye-tracking and EEG techniques can provide real-time insight into how figurative meanings are mapped during comprehension. Specifically, pairing online processing data with traditional behavioural measures holds promise for gaining a deeper understanding of the underlying sources of difficulty children experience with more nuanced pragmatic aspects of language learning (Falkum & Korder, 2020).

2.3 Assessments of Pragmatic Abilities in Children

Similar to other scientific domains, experimental pragmatics employs distinct paradigms and methodologies. In the context of researching children's pragmatic abilities, specialised methods are tailored to address targeted aspects of developmental processes. The bulk of empirical developmental data in experimental pragmatics is derived from **behavioural studies**, reflecting the field's historical alignment with psycholinguistics – a discipline dedicated to examining the psychological processes of language. While various experimental methodologies target specific pragmatic phenomena (refer to Bohn et al., 2023 for a comprehensive review), which prioritise theoretical analysis over clinical characterisation, there are relatively few batteries explicitly created to assess pragmatic abilities as a whole.

A common approach to assessing children's pragmatic abilities involves parental or teacher questionnaires that rate children's social communication skills. Tools such as the Pragmatic Language Skills Inventory (PLSI; Gilliam & Miller, 2006) or the Children's Communication Checklist (CCC-2; Bishop, 2006) are often employed to provide complementary insights beyond what can be observed during brief, standardised testing sessions. These checklists offer a more naturalistic assessment of a child's communicative abilities by gathering input from those who regularly interact with the child. The CCC-2, in particular, is translated into several languages and is used to assess children aged 4–16. This 70-item rating scale covers areas such as speech sounds, grammar skills, vocabulary, coherence, appropriateness of conversations, use of context, non-verbal communication, and social relationships. The CCC-2 offers a holistic view of a child's communication profile and is widely recognised for identifying pragmatic language impairments, as well as for screening children for autism spectrum disorder. These parental and teacher questionnaires are useful for capturing deficits that may be missed by other assessments that focus solely on isolated skills such as vocabulary or grammar.

One well-known battery of pragmatic assessment is the Assessment Battery for Communication (ABaCo; Sacco et al., 2008), originally developed to assess pragmatic abilities in patients affected by neuropsychological and psychiatric disorders, then standardised to assess pragmatic abilities in children (Bosco et al., 2012). It involves standardised tasks and real-life situations to comprehensively evaluate pragmatic inference abilities. For example, a study used the ABaCo to assess pragmatic abilities in children and adolescents in the autistic spectrum. The results showed that the ABaCo is effective in identifying and assessing pragmatic impairments in autistic individuals, with autistic participants scoring significantly lower on all ABaCo scales compared to matched controls, except for paralinguistic production (Angeleri et al., 2016). The ABaCo was initially designed for Italian speakers. Nevertheless, various sections of the battery have already been adjusted for use with English and Finnish speakers. Another widely used battery is the Test of Pragmatic Language (TOPL-2; Phelps-Terasaki & Phelps-Gunn, 2007) which is designed for individuals aged 8–18, and features a 43-item assessment, complemented by a 17-item version tailored for ages 6 and 7. This tool comprehensively evaluates seven fundamental aspects of pragmatics: physical context, audience, topic, purpose, visual–gestural cues, abstractions, and pragmatic evaluation. However, it may be more useful in assessing pragmatic language abilities in older children than in younger children (Hoffmann et al., 2013). This is likely because older children have more developed cognitive and language skills, allowing them to engage more effectively with the complex and abstract tasks required by the assessment.

The results of pragmatic language assessments are immensely useful for informing the planning of targeted interventions, particularly for children facing pragmatic impairments, such as those with autism (for a review, see Parson et al., 2017). Speech-language pathologists play a critical role in conducting these assessments. However, the complexity of evaluating pragmatic language skills demands careful consideration due to the multidimensional nature of these abilities. Pragmatic skills involve the integration of multiple interrelated linguistic and cognitive variables such as syntax, semantics, social understanding, and perspective-taking. They also interact with environmental factors like age, cognitive development level, and communication partners. Assessing a single component in isolation fails to capture this multidimensional profile. Current tools often measure discrete domains, but in natural communication, these domains interact fluidly and dynamically. Scoring individual areas provides an incomplete picture of overall pragmatic language ability. The ideal tool would provide a standardised evaluation of pragmatic language abilities as an integrated system rather than as separate components. While some endeavours have been made to address this need, there remains a significant gap in the development of comprehensive tools that can effectively capture the dynamic and interactive nature of pragmatic language skills in naturalistic contexts. This represents a critical research niche and an ongoing challenge for assessment development.

2.4 Pragmatic Language Abilities in the Adolescent Brain

The adolescent years mark an important phase of continued brain development (Crone & Dahl, 2012) that coincides with the refinement of socio-cognitive skills and pragmatic language abilities. During this period, teenagers refine their ability to engage in **turn-taking** conversations and maintain topic relevance. They also enhance their flexibility in adjusting language use according to social demands and dynamics within social groups. This linguistic development during **adolescence** facilitates more nuanced social and conversational skills which are essential for managing the growing intricacy of peer dynamics and social scenarios.

As adolescents navigate such an increasingly complex web of social relationships and environments, their capacity for pragmatic language undergoes significant changes, with pragmatic competence strongly shaping peer acceptance during this life stage. For example, Place and Becker (1991) investigated how pragmatic language skills relate to peer likeability ratings in elementary school students. They conducted an experiment with third- and fourth-grade girls who listened to audio recordings of hypothetical conversations between a peer and a school librarian. Across different scenarios, the target girl demonstrated behaviours related to requesting, turn-taking, responding promptly, and maintaining conversational coherence. These pragmatic skills were displayed either appropriately or inappropriately. Participants then rated how much they would like to interact with the target girl and provided descriptions of attractiveness, school ability, and popularity. The results showed that when the target girl exhibited pragmatic competence in the skills tested, she was viewed significantly more positively by listeners in terms of likeability, attractiveness, perceived academic ability, and popularity. Despite the topic relevance, investigations into the development and evolution of pragmatics specifically throughout adolescence remain comparatively under-explored relative to research on early childhood (see Section 2) and analyses of pragmatic behaviours in adult populations.

Amidst the aforementioned limited exploration of pragmatics development during adolescence, recent studies have shed light on key aspects of social cognition and language processing during this critical period. Arvidsson et al. (2022) explored the development of world knowledge-based audience design (AD) during adolescence, a fundamental aspect of social cognition involving tailoring utterances to the inferred knowledge of the listener. Through an online production task involving children entering adolescence (ages 11–12) and middle adolescents (ages 15–16), notable age-related disparities in AD emerge. While the younger cohort displayed inconsistency in adjusting their utterances based on assumed addressee knowledge, a marked enhancement in AD behaviour was observed among middle adolescents, underscoring a developmental progression. After the post-test survey, it was found that both age groups had similar beliefs about what the addressees knew regarding referents. However, the younger age group did not consistently adjust their utterances in real-time production based on these beliefs. Furthermore, while executive functions increased with age, it did not account for the age-related increase in AD performance, suggesting that the development of world knowledge-based AD in adolescence operates independently of executive functions development.

In another study, Asaridou et al. (2019) conducted a functional magnetic resonance imaging (fMRI) study to investigate how the brain processes pragmatic language in typically developing adolescents. Participants were presented with direct responses, indirect informative responses, and indirect affective responses to open-ended questions. Direct responses were simple answers to questions (e.g., Q: 'Where should we go for a nice family vacation?' A: 'Disneyland is a great place for little kids'), while indirect informative responses provided additional context (Q: 'Do you think the children will have fun on the trip?' A: 'Disneyland is a great place for little kids'). Indirect affective responses conveyed polite refusals, negative opinions, or face-saving intentions in response to emotionally charged questions (Q: 'Wouldn't it be great to go to Disneyland for our honeymoon?' A: 'Disneyland is a great place for little kids'). The researchers found greater brain activation in regions associated with Theory of Mind and language when adolescents analysed indirect responses that included negative opinions, refusals, or face-saving intentions, compared to those that simply provided more information. Specifically, activation was observed in the medial prefrontal cortex, temporoparietal junction, and temporal poles – areas linked to mentalising about others' perspectives and inferring speaker intention. These results lend support to previous evidence indicating adolescents have an enhanced sensitivity to social and affective cues relative to adults.

Thus, Theory of Mind likely plays a fundamental role in adolescents' pragmatic development, as suggested by Bosco et al.'s (2014) comprehensive study evaluating Theory of Mind progression from preadolescence through adolescence. Contrary to the prevalent notion that Theory of Mind reaches maturity in childhood, their research showed a continuous progression of Theory of Mind abilities into adolescence. However, the pace of enhancement varied across age groups, with a consistent trend observed between ages eleven and thirteen, followed by stabilisation. Despite this evidence of ongoing development, Bosco et al. also investigated the correlation between Theory of Mind development and communicative-pragmatic skills. Surprisingly, they found no significant age-related differences in adolescents' pragmatic performance. Nonetheless, further research is warranted to explore specific pragmatic competencies during adolescence. One promising avenue is exploring the influence of reading on cognitive and affective processes during this developmental stage. Research has already highlighted the potential for literary fiction to enhance Theory of Mind

(Kidd & Castano, 2013). By adopting a writerly stance, literary fiction stimulates presupposition, emphasising implicit meanings, subjectification, which portrays reality through the lens of the characters' consciousness, and multiple perspectives, allowing readers to perceive the world from various viewpoints simultaneously (Kidd & Castano, 2013: 377–378). These narrative techniques not only enhance Theory of Mind but might also cultivate pragmatic skills. By immersing readers in complex narratives that require them to infer characters' motivations, intentions, and emotions, literary fiction prompts a deeper understanding of human behaviour and social dynamics. Such evidence suggests potential long-term benefits of integrating literature more extensively into adolescent education and training programmes, especially in cultures where these aspects are traditionally viewed as less significant (i.e., educational systems heavily focused on STEM (Science, Technology, Engineering, Mathematics) subjects). The last Programme for International Student Assessment (PISA; OECD, 2023) survey, designed to offer a comprehensive international assessment of student knowledge and skills, shows a decline in the level of reading in many countries. 'Indeed the PISA 2022 results are unprecedented. Mean performance in OECD countries fell by [. . .] 10 score points in reading' and 'when it comes to reading, the odds of low performance are more than five times higher for disadvantaged students than their advantaged peers' (OECD, 2023: 44–45).

To conclude, adolescence is also crucial for acquiring sociocultural knowledge and refining the ability to use language effectively in social contexts. To date research should focus on how communication is changing in this new-era of adolescence, with the widespread use of social media platforms and the profound implications for their communication abilities. Unlike previous generations, who honed their social skills through direct interpersonal interactions, many teenagers now increasingly engage in social interaction and seek feedback through online channels (though it is important to consider potential cultural and class-specific differences; see Manago & McKenzie, 2022). While social media offers the allure of constant connectivity, excessive reliance on it as the primary mode of interaction may erode traditional face-to-face communication abilities. The focus on crafting a curated virtual persona and showcasing only the highlights of one's life may prioritise impression management over self-expression. Additionally, the anonymity afforded by social media platforms enables individuals to express their opinions without considering the nuances of tone or perspective, potentially impeding their conflict resolution skills. However, it is important to note that online behaviour necessitates individuals to anticipate how their posts will be perceived by others, suggesting potential evidence for Theory of Mind development.

2.5 Pragmatics in Multilingual Communities

Whether **bilingualism** or multilingualism (used interchangeably in this paragraph) arises from early acquisition of two languages or second language learning later in life, research consistently demonstrates cognitive advantages linked to *cognitive reserve* – our brain's ability to find alternative ways to complete tasks under increasing demand (a.o., Morales et al., 2013; see Garraffa et al., 2023 for an overview on the topic). Duncan et al. (2018) found speaking multiple languages may train brain areas involved in language and executive function, correlating with increased grey matter volume in healthy ageing adults and delayed cognitive symptoms in Alzheimer's patients.

While earlier works highlighted bilingualism's negative effects (e.g., reduced vocabulary, delayed language development), recent studies predominantly show advantages moderated by variables like acquisition age, L2 proficiency and **language immersion** (Valian, 2015). A main cognitive benefit relates to executive functions (meta-analysis in Adesope et al., 2010), plausibly because bilinguals must continuously inhibit their non-target language to regulate interference. This repeated switching and suppression may transfer to other cognitive domains requiring attention and control (Costa et al., 2008). Additionally, deciding which language to use with different interlocutors may aid Theory of Mind development in bilingual children (Greenberg et al., 2013), who outperform monolingual peers on Theory of Mind tasks (Siegal et al., 2010).

Researchers questioned if these Theory of Mind and executive function advantages confer pragmatic benefits. Studies found higher irony comprehension in bilingual versus monolingual children linked to Theory of Mind (Banasik & Podsiadło, 2016). However, *unbalanced bilinguals* (i.e., individuals who have significantly stronger proficiency in one language compared to the other) took longer with L2 irony due its cognitive demands (Bromberek-Dyzman & Rataj, 2016). Recently, researchers have explored the ease of processing scalar implicatures in bilingual populations; analysing this phenomenon in L2 has been considered useful for the theoretical debate. One might expect that if the computation of implicatures incurs a cognitive cost, *late bilinguals* (i.e., individuals who acquire a second language after early childhood) would be slower when processing them, while *balanced bilinguals* (i.e., individuals who have roughly equal proficiency in two languages across various contexts and domains of use) might have an advantage. On one side, some studies found an increase in pragmatic responses in bilinguals immersed daily in L2 (Slabakova, 2010). On the other side, a recent study on consecutive bilinguals revealed a decrease in pragmatic responses, due to the dual cognitive cost of implicature computation and test performance in L2 (Mazzaggio et al.,

2021), confirming that many factors come into play when it comes to pragmatics and bilingualism, including the type of test administration (written vs. oral), language immersion, and L2 proficiency.

The field of bilingualism and pragmatics remains ripe for further study, as languages and cultures interact in increasingly complex ways globally, as we will discuss in Section 5. In recent years, a new line of research has been exploring an understudied aspect of the relationship between bilingualism and pragmatic abilities: the impact of native speaker status on evaluations of others' speech. While most studies focused on the effects of bilingualism, this work shifts perspective to investigate monolingual speakers' expectations. Pioneering in this area are experiments by Fairchild and Papafragou (2018), revealing native speakers demonstrate greater 'pragmatic tolerance' towards under-informative utterances produced by non-natives. Further, the level of tolerance was linked to beliefs about the speaker's language proficiency: individuals believed to have lower abilities were judged more leniently in their under-informative remarks. These experiments provided novel insight into how pragmatic comprehension accommodates non-native language experience.

Discussions surrounding native speaker status are not new in English linguistics. A recent controversy involving a startup named Sanas,[2] which introduced AI technology to modify non-native speech of call centre employees to sound more American, has reignited these debates. This innovation sparked discussions and controversies regarding various aspects, including cultural implications, linguistic diversity, and ethical considerations.[3] At the forefront of the debate was the ethical dimension of altering individuals' speech patterns to conform to a specific cultural or linguistic standard. Critics argued that such technology could perpetuate cultural homogenisation and reinforce linguistic biases, potentially marginalising non-native speakers and disregarding the richness of linguistic diversity. On the other hand, proponents of the technology highlighted potential benefits such as improved customer service experiences and enhanced communication efficiency. Interestingly, they argued that providing tools to help non-native speakers improve their accents could potentially aid non-native employees in mitigating instances of customer misbehaviour, particularly from those who tend to exhibit rudeness towards individuals perceived as foreigners. Discussions delved into broader questions surrounding the role of technology in shaping language, culture, and identity. This includes the pragmatic competence necessary for understanding cultural nuances and adapting speech patterns. As

---

[2] www.sanas.ai/.

[3] See, for example: (1) www.businessinsider.com/ai-startup-sanas-accent-translation-technology-call-center-racism-2022-9; (2) https://theconversation.com/why-ai-software-softening-accents-is-problematic-197751.

AI technologies continue to advance and permeate various aspects of society, the Sanas debate served as a microcosm of larger societal conversations about the ethical implications of technological innovation. For a deeper exploration of the role of AI in mental healthcare, please refer to Section 5.3.

In conclusion, this section aimed at highlighting the dynamic nature of bilingualism and pragmatics, by providing insights into how language proficiency and cultural views interact to improve social interactions. Researchers and practitioners may help create inclusive workplaces where language variety is valued and communication obstacles are successfully overcome by promoting a greater grasp of pragmatic aspects of language.

3 Pragmatics across the Lifespan

This section comprehensively examines pragmatic language abilities across the lifespan and in various clinical contexts. It explores how pragmatics significantly impacts social functioning and outcomes. Ageing is associated with pragmatic declines, particularly in off-topic verbosity and non-literal language comprehension, which can promote feelings of loneliness and impede social communication. Neurological disorders disrupt pragmatics further. Research on dementia and amyotrophic lateral sclerosis (ALS) now increasingly evaluates nonliteral language due to its diagnostic and tracking importance for cognitive decline. Additionally, swearing is explored for its potent pragmatic functions and potential therapeutic benefits in healthcare settings. By integrating cognitive, linguistic, and social perspectives, this section provides novel insights into pragmatics' complex influences on social interactions and outcomes, with a particular focus into older age. It highlights pragmatics' significance for peer relationships, well-being, healthcare practices, and understanding neurological disorders.

3.1 Pragmatics in Healthy Ageing: Cognitive Ability and Social Use of Language

As outlined in the World Social Report 2023 by the United Nations Department of Economic and Social Affairs (DESA, 2023), population ageing is an irreversible global trend propelled by the demographic transition, characterised by extended life expectancies and smaller family sizes. This trend persists even in nations traditionally known for youthful populations. Projections indicate a substantial increase in the global population of individuals aged 65 years or older (the consensus among most researchers is that the designation of 'older adult' typically begins at the age of 65), expected to more than double from 761 million in 2021 to 1.6 billion by 2050. Notably, the demographic of individuals aged 80 years or older is expanding at an even faster rate. The concept of 'healthy ageing' emphasises the importance of maintaining functional ability as individuals age, facilitating their continued engagement in society and their quality of life. Pragmatics is particularly vulnerable to the effects of ageing, partly due to cognitive decline (Bambini et al., 2020b) and the specific social dynamics, including ageism and the erosion of social networks. Research indeed underscores a decline in pragmatic skills with physiological ageing, highlighting the complex nature of social skills development and decline throughout life (Messer, 2015), but also an age-related decline in mentalising abilities (Bernstein et al., 2011; Henry et al., 2013).

One extensively researched aspect is the occurrence of off-topic **verbosity** among older adults (Barnett et al., 2023). Numerous investigations into speech production have noted that older individuals often stray from the main topic, introducing irrelevant elements into conversations. Additionally, age-related disparities extend to the quantity, not just the quality, of speech: older adults tend to offer excessive information compared to what is essential for effective communication. A study conducted by Barnett et al. (2023) revealed that older adults tend to demonstrate greater tangentiality and egocentrism in their speech compared to younger counterparts. Notably, the study also found a significant association between loneliness and heightened tangentiality of speech, suggesting a link between the amount of off-topic information in everyday discourse and feelings of loneliness. The authors propose that this correlation may be attributed to older adults with high levels of off-topic verbosity inadvertently alienating potential social connections, thereby experiencing increased levels of loneliness. Another plausible explanation is that loneliness could be linked to both increased tangentiality and reduced speech quantity due to age-related declines in cognitive abilities, particularly in executive functions responsible for filtering irrelevant details and fostering generativity in speech. It is conceivable that loneliness and cognitive decline may mutually exacerbate each other, compounding the challenges faced by older individuals in social communication.

Targeted research within experimental pragmatics has revealed age-related declines across other various pragmatic domains. Multiple studies show older adults struggle with conversational demands like following discussions (Murphy et al., 2006) and comprehending non-literal language such as presuppositions (Domaneschi & Di Paola, 2019), metaphors (Mashal & Coblentz, 2014), proverbs (Nippold et al., 1997), humour (Bischetti et al., 2023), sarcasm (Phillips et al., 2015), and irony (Mazzaggio et al., 2023). Several cognitive factors appear influential, such as Theory of Mind (Bernstein et al., 2011), emotion recognition (Phillips et al., 2015), access to stored linguistic knowledge

(Craik & Bialystok, 2006), and executive functions (Bambini et al., 2021). However, precisely how these processes interact with pragmatic skills remains an active area of research.

Despite the perceived challenges, clinical pragmatics research offers hope. Studies show structured training programmes can effectively enhance pragmatic abilities in older adults. In one such study, Bambini et al. (2020b) evaluated a novel intervention called *PragmaCom*. The 'PragmaCom training is grounded in the Gricean model of communication (Grice, 1975), where communication is seen as a cooperative activity in which speakers try to offer a contribution to the ongoing conversation that is appropriate, in terms of sincerity (Maxim of Quality), amount of information (Maxim of Quantity), on-topic content (Maxim of Relevance), and clarity (Maxim of Manner)' (Bambini et al., 2020b: 2–3). Through exercises contextualised within stories depicting communication breakdowns, participants are prompted to recognise violations of maxims and discuss the underlying pragmatic mechanisms. Exercises cover both comprehension and production aspects, focusing on figurative language interpretation and appropriate discourse production. The intervention unfolds through four phases: detecting mismatches, reconstructing appropriate behaviour, generalising rules, and creating new contexts. Participants engage in activities such as identifying figurative meanings, analysing dialogue elements, selecting appropriate conversational exchanges, and creating new dialogues. Ecological items like newspaper articles or videos enrich sessions. Training is conducted in groups with individual engagement before group discussions to ensure active participation. Both a treatment group receiving *PragmaCom* training and a cognitive training group (targeting memory, speed of processing, and reasoning skills) engaged in weekly sessions over four weeks. Remarkably, both exhibited pragmatic gains like improved metaphor comprehension and conversational focus, indicating the potential for enhancing social communication in elderly individuals. Particularly noteworthy was the finding that the benefits derived from *PragmaCom* training were less contingent on individual participant characteristics, underscoring the broad applicability and effectiveness of such interventions.

Overall, these findings demonstrate the promising role of targeted clinical pragmatics interventions in addressing age-related declines. Training programmes, like *PragmaCom*, effectively improve pragmatic skills through structured training, supporting quality of life and social engagement for ageing populations. Ongoing exploration in this field offers hope for refining communication well-being among the elderly, a critical endeavour given that their challenges in social interaction can lead to loneliness, depression, and diminished social support.

3.2 The Role of Pragmatics in the Diagnosis of Dementia and Mild Cognitive Impairments

Communication is fundamental to human relationships and daily living. For this reason, as neurodegenerative disorders like **dementia** gradually erode language abilities, the facility to effectively interact with others is profoundly impacted. Performance on verbal tasks, and particularly semantic tasks, has been proposed as an important criterion for diagnosing Alzheimer's disease (AD) as well as **mild cognitive impairment** (MCI); recognising this significance is crucial as studies indicate the existence of a preclinical stage that may precede formal diagnosis by several years (Taler & Phillips, 2008). Moreover, in the initial stages of dementia, challenges may arise in the pragmatic aspects of language use and pragmatic language tests have been proposed for the early detection of cognitive decline in MCI and AD disease (Chakrabarty et al., 2023). For example, older adults with amnestic MCI (aMCI, i.e., MCI with memory loss) showed difficulties with verbal irony that were predicted by both Theory of Mind and executive functions. Specifically, Gaudreau et al. (2013) tested verbal irony comprehension and the relationship with first- and second-order belief attribution capacity in aMCI compared to healthy controls. aMCI had more difficulty correctly understanding verbal irony, compared with their healthy counterparts. Cognitive processes, more specifically second-order Theory of Mind and executive functions, were significantly associated with irony comprehension. Therefore, a pragmatic lens offers valuable insights for understanding a patient's declining language profile over time (to explore the topic further, see Davis et al., 2014).

Several research studies analysed nonliteral language abilities in AD, demonstrating difficulties in multiple aspects, like metaphors, irony, proverbs and idioms (for a review, see Rapp & Wild, 2011). For instance, in a groundbreaking study by Winner and Gardner (1977), individuals with brain lesions in the right hemisphere, left hemisphere, those with dementia, and a control group of lesion-free adults were subjected to a visual-verbal task assessing metaphor comprehension. Participants were presented with four images and tasked with selecting the one that best represented the metaphorical meaning of a given phrase. For instance, when presented with the metaphor 'A heavy heart can really make a difference', participants had to choose among options depicting the correct metaphorical interpretation (e.g., a person crying), the literal meaning (e.g., a person carrying a large red heart and collapsing under its weight), the adjective used in the metaphor (e.g., a weight), and the noun used in the metaphor (e.g., a red heart). Following image selection, participants were required to verbally explain the metaphor's meaning in their own words. The study's findings indicated a pronounced tendency among patients with right hemisphere damage to select the literal image (40 per cent), while individuals with AD also struggled significantly in choosing the image representing the correct metaphoric meaning. However, recent research suggests that AD patients may encounter greater difficulty with novel metaphors compared to conventionalised ones and that the impairment does not seem to be correlated with the severity of the cognitive disorder. Instead, it appears to be associated with deficits in executive functions and verbal reasoning (Amanzio et al., 2008).

AD patients struggle also with proverbs and idioms. Campanha and colleagues (2008) conducted a study examining the comprehension of popular Brazilian proverbs in a relatively large sample comprising AD patients and healthy controls. The results showed a significant decline in AD patients' ability to recognise, interpret, and abstract proverbs compared to the healthy control group. In the study by Papagno et al. (2003), participants with Alzheimer's disease (AD) were subjected to two experiments focusing on idiomatic expressions. The results revealed a significant correlation between poor performance on idiomatic tasks and performance on executive functions. The authors noted that AD patients frequently produced literal interpretations during idiom interpretation, suggesting a difficulty in suppressing the literal meaning in order to activate the intended figurative meaning.

It is not only figurative language that can be affected in dementia, but also the processing of implicatures. Spotorno et al. (2015) conducted a neuroimaging study to investigate the cognitive and neural underpinnings of scalar implicature comprehension in patients diagnosed with behavioural variant frontotemporal dementia (bvFTD); BvFTD is associated with progressive degeneration of the frontal and anterior temporal regions and causes impairments in theory of mind and executive functions (Pardini et al., 2013). Results from this experiment showed the bvFTD group had a tendency to interpret sentences based on their logical meaning rather than pragmatic implicatures, similarly to young children (see Section 2.2), and neuroimaging further revealed a correlation between experiment's performance and atrophy in the ventromedial prefrontal cortex. The authors concluded that the bvFTD group struggled with implicatures likely due to demands of generating alternative interpretations linguistically. However, when alternatives were provided visually in a further experiment, as in choice selection, difficulty was reduced. Thus, bvFTD impacts scalar implicature comprehension due to difficulty manipulating linguistic representations rather than conceptual representations of meaning. This underscores the importance of evaluating linguistic skills in the diagnosis not only of bvFTD but also of dementia in general.

In conclusion, individuals with AD often demonstrate impairments in understanding non-literal language. Verbal explanation tasks that assess nonliteral language ability are commonly used in clinical practice, as an inability to comprehend figurative expressions may indicate a deficit not fully captured by routine screening tests alone. As Rapp and Wild (2011) observed, both clinical practice and research frequently involve evaluating a patient's ability to interpret and articulate nonliteral language when assessing abstract thinking. This approach has a long-established tradition in psychiatry and neurology. However, despite its widespread use, there is a lack of consensus regarding the diagnostic reliability and specificity of this method for differentiating between subtypes of dementia. This presents a challenge, considering that deficits in comprehending figurative speech or pragmatic language more broadly can provide clinicians with meaningful insights for diagnosing and tracking the progression of cognitive impairment in AD and related conditions. Improved methods for reliably assessing nonliteral language comprehension could help differentiate between dementia subtypes and improve diagnostics.

3.3 Neurological Events and the Impact on Pragmatic Abilities

Pragmatic language abilities do not develop in isolation but rather emerge from a complex interplay between cognitive, linguistic, and neurological factors. As such, events that impact the normal functioning of the brain can potentially disrupt the use of pragmatic skills. A growing body of research has aimed to better understand how neurological disorders or injuries influence the pragmatic profile of individuals. Conditions that have been of particular interest include cerebral lesions resulting from strokes or traumatic injuries, as well as neurodegenerative diseases such as motor neuron disorders like Amyotrophic lateral sclerosis (ALS).

Lesions in different areas of the brain can result in distinct pragmatic difficulties due to disruption of the underlying networks. For example, right hemisphere damages (RHD) have been linked to several pragmatic difficulties (Parola et al., 2016), among other problems with **prosody** (Pell, 2006), with distinguishing lies from jokes (Winner et al., 1998), and with narrative skills (Marini et al., 2005). Left hemisphere damages (LHD) have been associated with more linguistic deficits that can also impact pragmatic competence, such as reduced vocabulary or difficulty with complex syntax. Cutica et al. (2006) analysed extra-linguistic aspects of pragmatic competence (communication performed solely through gestures) in healthy subjects, RHD patients, and LHD patients. A comparison of the performances of the three groups highlighted that, considering the overall score, both patient groups had significantly worse performances than healthy subjects. The authors argue that this confirms how both hemispheres significantly contribute to managing the mental representations and inferences involved in understanding a communicative act. However, there are differences between the performances of the two patient groups that suggest a different contribution of the two hemispheres; in fact, the LHL group showed fewer difficulties in approaching pragmatic acts compared to the RHL group. This result suggests that pragmatic ability, even when tested with extra-linguistic means, is based more, albeit not exclusively, on the right hemisphere. Similarly, in an experimental study, Kasher et al. (1999) assessed participants with LHD or RHD on their understanding of conversational implicatures based on Grice's maxims of conversation. Both a verbal test and a nonverbal test were administered. Notably, the results demonstrated that damage to either cerebral hemisphere led to impairments in comprehending implicatures. Although the behavioural outcomes were similar, the authors posited that this does not necessarily mean implicatures are processed identically by each hemisphere. Specifically, performance with implicatures correlated with distinct linguistic and neuropsychological measures for the LHD group versus the RHD group. This suggests that while both groups exhibited deficits, the underlying mechanisms may have differed according to the location of the brain lesion and the cognitive functions normally lateralised to that hemisphere.

Angeleri et al. (2008) instead examined pragmatic abilities in patients with traumatic brain injuries using the ABaCo battery (Sacco et al., 2008). The main results of the research revealed that traumatic brain injury patients had significant difficulties in pragmatic comprehension, particularly of deception and irony, compared to healthy adults. Production is also impaired compared to healthy participants: irony is the most difficult communicative act to produce. Patients also showed problems in understanding and producing paralinguistic aspects, remaining attached to the linguistic content expressed and neglecting the emotional meaning expressed through other modalities, such as prosody (i.e., intonation, rhythm, duration, stress that characterise our linguistic production). Finally, patients showed a pronounced tendency to persevere on the same topic during dialogue.

When considering ALS, it is crucial to recognise that it affects more than just motor abilities. A growing body of research shows that over half of individuals with ALS exhibit executive dysfunction or behavioural changes, with 15–20 per cent meeting criteria for frontotemporal dementia. Cognitive impairment in ALS extends beyond disruptions to frontal lobe–mediated functions alone. Studies have reported deficits in other cognitive domains like memory and confrontation naming (see Katerelos et al., 2023 for a review). Pragmatic skills seem also impaired in this population. Bambini et al. (2016) explored pragmatic impairments using the APACS battery

(Arcara & Bambini, 2016). ALS patients scored lower than controls on pragmatic tasks based on expressive (e.g., discourse) and receptive (e.g., metaphor and humour comprehension) tasks. Specific difficulties included the inability to maintain discourse topic and provide appropriate detail, communicating contextual elements, eye contact loss and fixed facial expressions during discourse. Comprehension problems included recalling implicit story details and interpreting non-literal meanings despite context. The authors also considered the role of executive functions and Theory of Mind. Executive functions significantly impacted production, while Theory of Mind significantly impacted comprehension. In other words, mental flexibility is fundamental for proper conversation management (topic/turn handling, salient information conveyance, repetition avoidance), while understanding others' behaviour is closely linked to comprehending a speaker's communicative intent, especially for non-literal language like metaphor and humour. Additional research by Bambini and colleagues (2020a) found further pragmatic deficits in ALS patients related to humour comprehension across diverse joke types, including impairments in understanding phonological jokes, mental jokes, and the mixed humour styles contained within the APACS assessment battery. The results shed light on pragmatic impairment as a relevant, understudied dimension of ALS cognition worthy of further consideration since pragmatic abilities are vital for everyday communication and social interaction.

In summary, neurological events can impact pragmatic language abilities. Pragmatic processing emerges from complex interactions between brain regions supporting cognitive, linguistic, and social functions. Events like strokes, traumatic injuries, neurodegenerative diseases, and more can disrupt these networks and underlying mechanisms. Continued investigation of pragmatic impairment across neurological disorders can provide insights into both typical development and rehabilitation approaches following brain damage or disease.

3.4 Abusive Language: The Power of Swearing

Swearing and abusive language have long fascinated researchers due to their controversial nature in social interactions. Various terms, such as expletives or epithets, are used to describe swear words, which encompass expressions considered offensive, inappropriate, or objectionable within specific social contexts (a.o., Fägersten, 2012: 3). Swearing is recognised as a powerful tool in social interactions, capable of eliciting strong reactions ranging from offence and insult to fostering positive relational dynamics (for a review, Stapleton &

Fägersten, 2023; Vingerhoets et al., 2013). While its use may occasionally lead to negative outcomes, such as hurt feelings or strained relationships, swearing also has the potential to foster intimacy and connection among individuals. In certain contexts, the mutual exchange of profanity can even cultivate a sense of shared identity and camaraderie, strengthening social bonds and fostering a sense of belonging within a group.

Swearing involves a complex interplay of brain regions. The emotional response triggered by swearing is initiated by the amygdala and basal ganglia, which are part of the brain's primitive core. These regions are involved in emotional processing and threat detection. Swearing then engages the cortex associated with higher cognitive functions like language production. Research suggests that swear words are processed differently in the brain compared to regular language, originating from deeper, more primitive and emotional areas (Pinker, 2007). Damage to these structures can result in coprolalia, a condition characterised by frequent and uncontrollable utterances of swear words, which is also observed as a symptom in some patients with Tourette's syndrome (about 10 per cent; Freeman et al., 2009), wherein swearing manifests as an uncontrollable tic alongside other sudden, repetitive, non-rhythmic movements or utterances. Significantly, swearing persists also in severe aphasia when other language is lost, indicating separate neural representation from non-taboo words (Van Lancker & Cummings, 1999). A recent fMRI study examined how monolinguals and highly proficient bilinguals processed taboo versus non-taboo words (Sulpizio et al., 2019). Behaviourally, non-taboo words elicited similar offensiveness ratings across languages, but taboo words seemed less offensive in the foreign language compared to the native language. Neurologically, language modulated activity in specific regions, with taboo words eliciting stronger activation, possibly due to weaker word-form to semantics associations in a second language. However, this framework only explains automatic impulsive insults processed by right-hemisphere, basal ganglia, and amygdala circuits as unified blocks lacking semantic meaning, like 'Dickhead!' More elaborate comparative insults, requiring reasoning, controlled inference, and linguistic choice, challenge this simplistic model. While swearing involves primitive emotional circuits, intentional propositional insults demonstrate higher-order linguistic and cognitive functions beyond this framework. A comprehensive understanding requires considering both impulsive and elaborated swearing behaviours.

Recent clinical research is beginning to explore the potential advantages of swearing (Hay et al., 2024). Washmuth and Stephens (2022) highlight how swearing can have a positive impact on patient outcomes when used strategically within a biopsychosocial approach to care. Reviewing the literature, the authors suggest how swearing can be strategically utilised to improve patient outcomes in physical therapy by leveraging its potential benefits. Swearing has indeed been shown to have various effects. It can increase pain tolerance and pain thresholds by distracting individuals from painful stimuli, making it more tolerable to engage in physical activities that may cause discomfort. This enhanced pain tolerance could allow patients to participate more fully in rehabilitation exercises. However, recently, there has been evidence that invented 'swear' words do not yield comparable pain relief effects to conventional swearing. Although these newly created 'swear' words were found to elicit similar levels of heightened emotion and humour ratings as swearing, they were ineffective in alleviating pain onset or increasing pain tolerance (Stephens & Robertson, 2020). In the same study, the authors firstly explored whether distraction mediates the pain-alleviating effects of swearing. Findings suggest that distraction is not a contributing factor to the mechanism by which swearing mitigates pain. Instead, data propose that swearing exerts its influence on pain relief through an alternative pathway, potentially involving heightened emotional arousal (Stephens & Robertson, 2020).

Moreover, uttering swear words during physical tasks has been associated with greater levels of peak power, average power, and maximal force development, suggesting that swearing may enhance physical performance during exercises or rehabilitation activities also reducing the social pain. Strengthening performance could contribute to faster recovery time. Additionally, swearing can create tighter human bonds and enhance the therapeutic alliance between patients and physical therapists. A positive therapeutic alliance is crucial for effective patient care and can lead to better treatment outcomes. A recent case study of a 44-year-old female provided evidence that repeating a swear word out loud strengthened the therapeutic alliance, improved physical performance, and decreased pain. Swearing was formally incorporated into her care plan, and she swore aloud during challenging interventions. She reported swearing was a fun distraction that boosted her confidence. Both patient and therapist reported a strong alliance (Washmuth et al., 2023).

While swearing remains controversial in healthcare, these findings suggest it may have strategic benefits within physical therapy if applied judiciously and with patient consent. This is particularly evident in emerging trends such as *rage yoga*, where swearing and screaming are integrated into yoga practices to help individuals release stress, cultivate calmness, and enhance fitness levels through unconventional means, including the expression of raw emotions and the use of dark humour.[4] This approach offers a safe space for individuals to

---

[4] www.rageyoga.com/.

vent frustration and anger in a constructive manner, blending traditional yoga techniques with a more relaxed and humorous atmosphere. However, research has yet to study the specific effects and benefits of rage yoga.

This section has examined the complex role of swearing in social interactions and its potential therapeutic benefits. Swearing, while controversial, can foster emotional expression, social bonding, and intimacy. Neurologically, it involves distinct brain pathways and persists even in some language disorders. Clinical research indicates that strategic swearing can enhance physical therapy by increasing pain tolerance, improving performance, and strengthening patient–therapist relationships. More research is still needed, but swearing shows promise as an adjunct tool to improve outcomes when used appropriately and within a caring, therapeutic relationship. Overall patient well-being and comfort should always be the top priority in any decisions around incorporating swearing into care plans.

4 Pragmatics in the Clinic

Understanding pragmatic language impairments across various neurodevelopmental and neurological conditions is essential for targeted intervention and support. This chapter explores pragmatic challenges in autism spectrum disorder (ASD), attention deficit hyperactivity disorder (ADHD), multiple sclerosis (MS), and addiction. In ASD, deficits in social communication and interaction are pervasive, impacting language acquisition and pragmatic abilities. Individuals with ADHD face difficulties in sustaining attention and regulating impulsivity, affecting their pragmatic language skills. MS patients experience disruptions in communication due to motor impairments and cognitive deficits, leading to challenges in interpreting ambiguities and metaphors. In addiction, narratives and metaphors shape communication patterns, reflecting the complexities of psychological and physical dependence. Through the clarification of these pragmatic deficits, customised treatments may be created to cater to the specific requirements of each person affected by these disorders, therefore enhancing their academic, social, and emotional well-being.

4.1 Pragmatic Abilities in the Atypical Continuum: The Case of Autism Spectrum Disorder

In the discipline of clinical linguistics, studies on autism spectrum disorders (ASD) are perhaps the most fruitful (Kissine, 2021). This is partly because pragmatic skills are a fundamental area of weakness in ASD. The term 'autism' (from the Greek word αυτός, meaning *self*) was first used in relation to schizophrenia in 1911 by the Swiss psychiatrist Eugen Bleuler. He was referring to a symptom in which people withdraw from social reality and become inwardly focused. The evolution of the term occurred in the 1940s, when researchers Leo Kanner and Hans Asperger independently employed the same term to describe a distinct set of developmental disorders. One striking portrayal captures the essence of their social challenges: 'The most impressive thing is his detachment and inaccessibility. He walks as if he were in a shadow, lives in his own world where he cannot be reached. No sense of relationship with people' (Kanner, 1943: 236). Kanner's observations highlighted the profound detachment and communication difficulties in autistic children, and these disorders, now collectively known as autism spectrum disorders, are characterised by persistent deficits in social communication and interaction, encompassing anomalies in socio-emotional reciprocity, non-verbal communicative behaviours, and challenges in developing and maintaining relationships across diverse social contexts, as outlined in the *DSM-5*.

The acquisition of language in autistic children usually involves delays in the early stages of development but may also not appear at all. Several children on the spectrum present with a deficiency in expressive language, with a noteworthy majority demonstrating language output characterised by **echolalia** and stereotyped forms, defined as the persistent and invariant repetition of motor or verbal sequences. Despite variations in phenotypic severity and the diversity of linguistic and intelligence profiles (Schaeffer et al., 2023), pragmatics stands out as the linguistic domain most consistently and universally affected in autism. This observation holds true even for individuals scoring within the normal range on IQ tests and exhibiting normative structural language skills.

Starting from Kanner's studies (1943), for example, several experiments have highlighted difficulties in the use of personal pronouns (Naigles et al., 2016) and **deixis** (Mizuno et al., 2011) by autistic children. To date, this difficulty seems to go beyond a general language acquisition delay, with multiple cognitive, social, and linguistic factors at play (Naigles et al., 2016). Mazzaggio and Shield (2020) tested autistic children on the production of first- and second-person singular pronouns, deciding to compare children with the same verbal IQ but not chronological age because previous studies suggested that language skills play a more important role in pronoun production. The results demonstrated that autistic children, compared to typically developing children, had greater difficulty with all tested pronouns, despite being older. Furthermore, children on the autistic spectrum showed a greater tendency to produce proper names rather than pronouns. Thanks to data in Italian, a language in which pronouns can be omitted (i.e., a **pro-drop language**), it was possible to observe that autistic children have a greater tendency to verbally produce the pronoun rather than omit it when contextually inferable. Not omitting a pronoun when redundant and tending to talk about themselves and the interlocutor with names instead of pronouns can be seen as a violation of a conversational maxim: not providing more information than is required (Grice, 1975). Also, Surian et al. (1996) demonstrated that autistic children unlike typically developing children and children with specific language impairment (SLI), have difficulties in detecting pragmatic violations across various conversational maxims as defined by Grice. These maxims include Quantity, Quality, Relation, and Politeness. In their study, children listened to short conversational exchanges where one speaker's response in each exchange violated a specific maxim. Autistic children performed at a chance level in identifying these violations, indicating a significant deficit in pragmatic understanding compared to their typically developing and SLI peers. This deficit was linked to impairments in their Theory of Mind abilities, which are essential for interpreting and generating appropriate conversational implicatures. The study also highlighted that while autistic children could detect grammatical errors, they struggled with pragmatic violations, suggesting that their communicative challenges are more deeply rooted in social cognition rather than language competence alone. Other works confirmed difficulties in autistic individuals, including challenges with inappropriate topic shifting and conversational difficulties, pedantic speech, and difficulties with figurative language (Lampri et al., 2023; Ying Sng et al., 2018).

Several studies provide evidence for a robust connection between pragmatic competence, social skills, and Theory of Mind (Tager-Flusberg, 2000), and targeted pragmatic deficits in the autistic population have been attributed to an underdeveloped Theory of Mind (Cardillo et al., 2020). However, as experimental pragmatic research on autistic populations has surged in recent years, the verbal intelligence quotient, representing linguistic skills, has emerged as a frequently identified critical factor, often acting as a compensatory mechanism for pragmatic challenges. Specifically, 'when autistic individuals use and interpret language in context, they do so without projecting themselves in the minds of their conversational partners' (Kissine, 2021: 7), and this happens, among other phenomena, for metaphors and indirect speech acts comprehension (Marocchini et al., 2022).

An over-studied example of a pragmatic phenomenon in which language seems to have a compensatory strategic function is **scalar implicatures** (Foppolo & Mazzaggio, 2024). Pijnacker et al. (2009) tested Dutch autistic adults. The task involved presenting logically true but pragmatically false sentences containing the scalar quantifier 'some' (e.g., some sparrows are birds) and the connective 'or' (e.g., zebras have black or white stripes). For example, consider the statement 'Some sparrows are birds'. Logically, this statement is true because sparrows are indeed a type of bird. However, the use of the term 'some' implies that there may be sparrows that are not birds, which is pragmatically false since all sparrows are birds. Unexpectedly, the results showed similar responses in the two groups: overall, the pragmatic responses of the autistic group were not significantly different from those observed in the control group. However, the researchers found a correlation between pragmatic responses and verbal intelligence: the higher the verbal intelligence, the more frequent the pragmatic responses. According to the authors, autistic participants may use their verbal intelligence to compensate for pragmatic difficulties. Despite this, it cannot be ignored that recent studies with contrasting results (i.e., difficulties with scalar implicatures) have appeared, both regarding autistic children (Mazzaggio et al., 2019) and adults with marked autistic traits (Mazzaggio & Surian, 2018).

In conclusion, rather than assuming a broad pragmatic incapacity in autistic individuals, it is imperative to adopt a more nuanced perspective. The spectrum nature of autism suggests that performances may vary based on the severity of the disorder. An illustrative case is a recent study by Panzeri and colleagues (2022), which scrutinised the processing of ironic compliments and criticisms. In this study, autistic children were compared to two age- and language-matched groups of typically developing children. The investigation aimed to identify factors predicting irony comprehension performance. Results revealed that autistic children did not demonstrate comparable performance to controls in comprehending both subtypes of verbal irony, and their performance correlated with both Theory of Mind and linguistic abilities. The most intriguing finding was the detection of a **bimodal distribution**, indicating two distinct profiles among autistic participants regarding verbal irony comprehension. The majority (about 70 per cent) struggled with almost all questions assessing irony understanding, while the remaining children answered all twelve questions correctly. Such a clear-cut distribution was absent in the control groups. These findings underscore the considerable heterogeneity within autism, emphasising the need for a more thorough investigation into individual profiling among autistic participants (Kissine, 2021). Clinicians and educators must adopt a comprehensive understanding of each individual's pragmatic strengths and weaknesses, acknowledging the variability within the spectrum and ensuring that intervention strategies are adapted to address the specific needs of each person.

Let us conclude this section, mentioning that the subjective character of communication skills may make it difficult to define pragmatic weaknesses. For instance, determining what constitutes a 'difficulty' in pragmatic processing involves subjective judgements about the adequacy of an individual's ability to adapt communication to various contexts. Similar to this, 'adhering to conversational norms' is made more difficult by the fact that these standards aren't always accepted and might change depending on the situation and culture. As discussed previously in Section 2.3, standardised assessments play a crucial role in this domain despite these challenges. These assessments are meticulously designed and validated to provide objective evaluations of pragmatic skills across diverse populations. They employ empirical data from large participant samples to offer structured assessments that capture critical components of communication skill.

Researchers and practitioners may more accurately identify communication problems, track progress, and customise therapies to improve pragmatic processing in real-world situations by incorporating these validated measures into clinical practice. Crucially, research has shown that pragmatic training programmes are quite successful in encouraging significant gains in pragmatic abilities, also in people on the autistic spectrum (Parsons et al., 2017).

4.2 Pragmatic Language Impairment in ADHD

Attention deficit hyperactivity disorder (ADHD) is a neurodevelopmental disorder characterised by profound impacts on an individual's social functioning and interpersonal relationships. ADHD is characterised by a variety of symptoms, prominently featuring impulsivity, hyperactivity, and persistent challenges with sustained attention (DSM-5, 2013). This condition is particularly noteworthy for its prevalence among children and adolescents, constituting one of the most commonly diagnosed disorders in these age groups (Bitsko et al., 2022). Beyond childhood, ADHD can continue into adulthood and have an impact on a variety of areas of a person's life, including interactions with others and their career.

Language impairments are becoming more widely recognised in this population, and comorbidity is prevalent with difficulties in expressive, receptive, and pragmatic language skills (Korrel et al., 2017). These challenges have been mainly explained as linked to limitations in executive functions (Cummings, 2017), suggesting also a causal relationship with difficulties observed in Theory of Mind (Mary et al., 2016). However, other theories aim to explain the pragmatic difficulties associated with ADHD (Carruthers et al., 2022: 1939). One perspective posits that pragmatic language deficits naturally correlate with fundamental symptoms of ADHD, such as response latency, excessive verbalisation, conversational impatience, and intrusion. Conversely, hyperactivity/impulsivity and concentration impairments that impact verbal and non-verbal communication could be the secondary cause of pragmatic difficulties. Another viewpoint is that ADHD symptoms may make it harder to practice social communication skills, which might lead to pragmatic language difficulties. Additionally, the pragmatic language issues that are so important for successful social interactions may be the direct cause of poor social functioning in ADHD. Importantly, pragmatic difficulties are not consistently correlated with overall linguistic abilities (Väisänen et al., 2014). This finding implies that standardised language tests focused on structural aspects of language like grammar and vocabulary may not adequately capture the nuanced pragmatic challenges experienced by individuals with ADHD. It suggests pragmatic language abilities should be evaluated separately through **Discourse Analyses** and social communication measures in order to develop a comprehensive understanding of the communication strengths and limitations present in ADHD (see Section 5 for a focus on pragmatics and discourse analysis during clinical interactions). Recognising pragmatic impairments despite average linguistic skills is critical for guiding appropriate intervention and accommodations to maximise social, emotional, and academic well-being.

Several review papers analysed the pragmatic language skills of individuals with ADHD and consistently affirmed and detailed a range of difficulties (Carruthers et al., 2022; Green et al., 2014; Korrel et al., 2017). For example, ADHD children frequently have trouble striking an appropriate equilibrium when it comes to language use, which can result in problems like over-talking and dominating conversations with a hostile style. Moreover, it becomes very difficult to keep conversations on topic, and they have trouble changing their communication style to suit various contexts. They could make unrelated remarks that deviate from the topic at hand and cause the conversation to go off course. They frequently argue and interrupt the conversational partner, which ruins the natural flow of the conversation and makes it difficult to establish a consistent and productive communication rhythm over time. Understanding nonliteral language, such as irony and sarcasm, is also difficult for ADHD children. For example, Caillies and coll., 2014 tested French ADHD children on irony comprehension, evidencing how ADHD children provided poorer explanations for the ironic comments compared to controls.

When it comes to storytelling, stories of ADHD individuals might not have the same cohesiveness and easy flow as those of other children their age; the former tend to make more errors and inaccuracies, for example by introducing extraneous information or ambiguous references, and are less sensitive to the structural properties of stories (Lorch et al., 1999). Miranda-Casas et al. (2004) looked at both ADHD children and those without ADHD in a comparative investigation of narrative sequences incorporating real-life events. The goal was to evaluate the coherence and grammatical structures used in these stories. The results showed differences: the ADHD group used fewer **conversational markers**, which are crucial for organising utterances. Additionally, they had a greater frequency of topic changes in conversations, adding irrelevant material. The authors concluded that stories from children with ADHD present more comprehension difficulties, requiring the listener to take on a more active role to make up for the lack of coherent information.

These children are essentially facing a unique set of communication barriers that call for a sophisticated strategy for successful intervention to make them less unpopular and rejected by peers. It takes more than just addressing their inclination to talk too much or forget what they are talking about to help them negotiate the complexities of social communication; rather, it involves customising support to promote sincere and meaningful relationships. Indeed, recent research, exemplified by a systematic review (Fox et al., 2020), emphasises the efficacy of social skills interventions with peer interactions, highlighting their success in enhancing play skills, diminishing negative behaviours, and improving communication, including pragmatic language abilities, collaboration, and joint participation. This underscores the promising potential of focused interventions to effectively target and mitigate social and pragmatic difficulties. Key components of these interventions involve making environmental adjustments to foster successful interactions, providing immediate feedback on inappropriate behaviour, systematic teaching of social skills and problem-solving, and incorporating role models to reinforce positive behaviours.

4.3 Communication Deficits in Multiple Sclerosis: Cognitive and Social Cognition

Understanding communicative abilities in individuals with multiple sclerosis (MS) is essential for comprehensive management and support of this chronic disease. MS affects the **central nervous system** and is believed to stem from an autoimmune response where the body mistakenly attacks itself. The impact of multiple sclerosis varies significantly between individuals, leading to unpredictable and fluctuating symptoms across physical, cognitive, and communicative domains. While some may experience mild effects, others face greater challenges in vision, mobility, or communication due to disruptions in signalling between the brain and body. Importantly, communication is commonly impaired in MS through both motor and cognitive pathways, underscoring the need for comprehensive assessment and support of language abilities. Challenges are often manifested as motor impairments like **dysarthria** that impact speech production. Additionally, considerable cognitive impairment is well documented, negatively impacting attention, processing speed, memory, and linguistic skills central to effective interaction like word retrieval (Plotas et al., 2023; Renauld et al., 2016).

Pragmatic skills, such as interpreting ambiguities and metaphors, reconstructing sentences, and making inferences, have also been found to be impaired in multiple sclerosis patients (Lethlean & Murdoch, 1997). For example, Lethlean and Murdoch assessed how well multiple sclerosis patients – with ages ranging from twenty-six to seventy-six years – could identify different meanings of ambiguous sentences. One simple sentence they used was 'Bob did not blame the girl as much as her mother', which contains a surface structure ambiguity. This sentence could mean either that Bob blamed the girl less than he blamed her mother, or that the level of blame the mother placed on the girl was greater than what Bob placed on her. Some patients in the study struggled to provide distinct alternative interpretations for sentences like these, demonstrating the challenges this population can face with pragmatically understanding implicit or ambiguous meanings in language.

In research by Arrondo et al. (2010), people with multiple sclerosis were tasked with a thirty-minute discourse on their life histories. The verbal production was then transcribed and examined, and the results showed several quantitative differences from the control group. These differences included a diminished total number of words produced, a decreased mean sentence length, a reduced maximum sentence length, and an elevated number of words produced by the evaluator. Moreover, the discrepancy in the number of words spoken by the evaluator between patients and control subjects correlated with executive functions, as assessed by the Paced Auditory Serial Addition Task (Gordon & Zillmer, 1997) and phonetic fluency. It was indeed observed that the evaluator needed to engage more with cognitively impaired patients to sustain the conversation, signifying that these individuals face challenges in transitioning between topics and exhibit difficulties in planning their discourse to circumvent periods of silence. The authors claim that if people with multiple sclerosis receive ongoing feedback, they shouldn't have any trouble interacting with others in normal scenarios. They could, however, find it difficult to autonomously produce complicated discourses. This deficiency, which affects the general coherence and social application of language, might be characterised as pragmatic in nature.

In recent studies, specific experiments were designed to evaluate pragmatic skills in individuals with multiple sclerosis. Carotenuto et al. (2018a) conducted research involving patients and healthy controls, employing the Assessment of Pragmatic Abilities and Cognitive Substrates (APACS), a standardised pragmatic test for the Italian-speaking population (Arcara & Bambini, 2016). The findings confirmed pragmatic impairments in multiple sclerosis patients, as they exhibited poorer performance compared to controls across various sections of the APACS test. Patients specifically showed deficiencies in discourse levels, including both production and understanding. More precisely, individuals struggled to provide enough information, especially in discourse production, and showed signs of breakdown in pragmatic abilities when it came to activities testing understanding of nonliteral language (such as humour and figurative language). The overall scoring revealed that pragmatic impairments are widespread in the MS community, with about 55 per cent of patients performing below the 5th percentile. In a further study, Carotenuto et al. (2018b) confirmed impaired pragmatic abilities in multiple sclerosis patients. Their findings indicated a robust correlation between these impairments and alterations in neural connectivity, particularly within the bilateral temporoparietal regions, specifically with the Geschwind's area and the paracingulate cortex.

In conclusion, individuals with multiple sclerosis exhibit deficits in both pragmatic and structural aspects of language production. These challenges are associated with cognitive impairment, specifically executive dysfunction, though it is important to acknowledge the potential contribution of dysarthria to these differences (Arrondo et al., 2010).

4.4 Pragmatic Language in People with Addiction

Exploring the intersection of addiction and pragmatic communication is essential for gaining insights into the complex dynamics surrounding psychological and/or physical dependence on substances or behaviours. Addiction can manifest itself in different forms, including addiction to psychoactive substances (such as drugs or alcohol) or behavioural addiction (such as gambling, internet, sex, or food). The psychological and physical dependence that characterises addiction leads to distinctive patterns of thinking, feeling, and behaving. For example, addicted individuals may employ pragmatic strategies, consciously or not, to justify and normalise their addictive actions. Their language could minimise harm, exaggerate benefits, discount social consequences, and portray addiction as a lack of willpower rather than a complex medical condition. Over time, addiction can reshape pragmatic competence by influencing how information is selectively attended to, remembered, and discussed. This is reflected in the narratives people construct about their addiction experiences.

Through storytelling, individuals aim to make sense of and come to terms with their condition; for this reason, **narrative research** has emerged as a valuable tool in recent years for investigating various aspects of cognitive functions, emotion regulation, self-control, and the structure of the Self (Pennebaker, 2000), which may be particularly important for those with addiction seeking to gain insight into their behaviours and motivations. Indeed, the narrative tool allows individuals to organise their life events and define themselves as intentional agents, reconstructing their experiences in line with their sense of Self. This is particularly relevant since, in recent years, a considerable body of research has offered increasing evidence that various cognitive abilities linked to storytelling, including Theory of Mind, recalling past events (Episodic Memory), envisioning the future (Episodic Future Thinking), and navigating spatial environments (Mental Space Travel), exhibit notable functional similarities and depend on a shared core brain network (Adornetti et al., 2021).

Individuals struggling with substance use disorders or other addictions frequently demonstrate peculiar communication patterns, narratives, and pragmatic approaches that are shaped by a diverse set of influences. Metaphors, in particular, are a rhetorical device often used in addiction narratives. Traditionally, within classical studies, metaphors were mainly examined as a literary and poetic technique used by authors and poets to enrich their writing. However, in their 1980 book *Metaphors We Live By*, Lakoff and Johnson revolutionised how metaphor is perceived and took a novel approach by exploring how metaphor is unconsciously embedded in everyday speech. They proposed that metaphor is not merely an ornamental device but rather a fundamental aspect of the human conceptual system, arising inevitably from how our brains categorise and reason about the world. On a deeper level, they argue that our entire conceptual framework and thought processes inherently involve metaphorical elements.

This groundbreaking perspective shifted studies of metaphors away from its rhetorical usage alone (see also Section 5.2). By their nature, metaphors allow indirect or implicit communication that can help address deeply felt emotions or sensitive topics. They provide an oblique lens through which to view addiction-related experiences, observations, and insights. Metaphors may be consciously or subconsciously employed to compare the addiction journey and its affliction to concepts more palatable than a direct acknowledgement of destructive behaviours and their harms (Shinebourne & Smith, 2010).

Metaphors, in the context of addiction, commonly represent the addiction journey or recovery process. Substances or behaviours may be portrayed as 'controlling forces' that must be outmanoeuvred or overcome. For example, addiction is metaphorically described as a 'battlefield' or an 'incurable illness', and recovery is an 'arduous' process that gets people 'back to life' (Shinebourne & Smith, 2010). Metaphors like these can soften the harsh realities of destructive addiction by framing it in more culturally appropriate terms. They may also help one psychologically distance oneself from the stigma of the condition. Malvini Redden et al. (2013) conducted a qualitative study to explore themes and issues related to substance abuse, recovery, and medication-assisted treatment. The researchers analysed data obtained from focus group interviews with English-speaking participants. The metaphorical language used by participants in the focus groups provided insights into their perspectives, and their metaphorical descriptions often reflected the social stigmas surrounding drug use and medication-assisted treatment. As deeply analysed in the paper (Malvini Redden et al., 2013: 959), when recounting past drug use, the discussions took on a more positive, nostalgic, and even wistful tone compared to descriptions of present recovery experiences. In describing their active addiction, participants used vivid language to talk about activities like procuring and using drugs. Their language depicted a sense of agency in behaviours like 'hustling', 'scoring', and 'shooting'. In contrast, their discussions of entering treatment lacked similar framing and did not portray themselves as active agents in that process: recovery was portrayed in lonely, bleak terms as 'tedious', 'difficult', and 'boring'. Once in treatment as well, the participants' language took on a more passive tone that conveyed an absence of control or influence. During periods of active addiction, terms like 'taking' and 'choosing' indicated a sense of power and will over their actions. However, when discussing recovery, people depicted experiences where outside forces acted upon them, such as being 'saved by an angel', 'cleaned', or 'detoxed' from substances. The language used by participants portrayed their recovery experience in terms of avoidance rather than active engagement, with discussions focused on 'staying away from drugs', 'walking away from temptation', and 'hiding from trouble' rather than taking steps towards positive goals. Additional language, like being ensnared by 'liquid handcuffs', implies that recovery involves ceding personal decision-making and control. Through analysing these metaphors, the researchers gained an understanding of tacit cognitive challenges. Metaphors serve as a shorthand for experience and implicitly shape how individuals conceive of addiction and recovery.

Ultimately, a complex interplay of psychological and social factors embedded within individuals' life experiences shapes distinctive patterns in how people with addictions utilise communication regarding their journey. Different types of substance use disorders likely contribute to notable variations in the narratives put forth. In a study comparing narrative styles between individuals with gambling disorder (GD) and substance use disorder (SUD), Canali et al. (2021) found some notable differences. Those with GD expressed a stronger sense of agency, or ability to make choices and act. They also conveyed higher levels of passivity, or lack of control over outcomes. Additionally, their accounts reflected a more external locus of control, meaning they attributed outcomes to external factors like luck rather than their own actions. Those with GD are also presented as more externally motivated or driven by rewards and social approval from others. These differences are analysed as a dissociation between cognition, emotions, motivations, and actions for those with behavioural addictions – compared to SUD – where subjects struggle more to recognise themselves as 'addicts' due to fears of social stigma surrounding that label. Understanding these nuanced differences can guide more empathy-based, tailored approaches to assessment and treatment. Indeed, Lyddon et al. (2001) analysed how, in the counselling context, a counsellor's ability to recognise and appropriately utilise their client's metaphorical expressions can greatly facilitate the therapeutic process. By showing attentiveness to the metaphors clients generate, counsellors are better able to convey empathic understanding in a way that communicates both verbal and emotional comprehension. This helps to establish the collaborative working alliance that is so crucial.

Thurnherr (2021) explores a complementary perspective, illustrating how counsellors can use metaphors like the 'garden' to engage and empower clients, demonstrating the versatile application of metaphorical techniques in therapeutic settings. According to Thurnherr, the metaphor of a 'garden' represents the internal landscapes of his clients, whereby their good traits are compared to blooming flowers and their negative traits are compared to weeds that need to be managed. In addition to making difficult psychological ideas easier to understand, this metaphorical framework promotes reflection and cooperation in therapeutic settings. Depending on their own requirements for therapy and how they view themselves, clients may react to this metaphor in different ways. Counsellors who are skilled at using metaphors can help clients engage more deeply and foster transformational progress inside the therapeutic partnership.

To sum up, exploring addiction through the lens of pragmatic communication one may discover how individuals construct narratives to navigate and understand their dependency on substances or behaviours. These narratives often employ metaphors to reshape perceptions of addiction, framing it as a battle or illness to be overcome. Clinicians may be able to better understand the complicated interactions between identity, stigma, and therapeutic involvement in addiction treatment by analysing these language and story techniques. Comprehending these dynamics improves compassionate methods customised to each patient's story, leading to better therapeutic results.

5 Pragmatics in the Healthcare Practice

Language plays a visible role in healthcare, both as a medical symptom and as a resource for practice. This section delves into the latter aspect, particularly in relation to the growing prevalence of social (pragmatic) communication disorder (SPCD). Given that rehabilitation professionals working with SPCD patients hail from diverse disciplines such as speech-language therapists (SLTs) and psychologists, it is not uncommon for various approaches and communication styles to be employed in addressing SPCD. Moreover, SPCD is influenced by a myriad of factors, including culture, gender, spoken languages, socio-economic status, psychosocial factors, and interpersonal relationships. These elements significantly impact the assessment of pragmatic communication, thereby affecting the development of clinical protocols. This section explores several facets of studying pragmatics in healthcare, including the utilisation of metaphorical language in healthcare practice, intercultural considerations, and the imperative of assessing conversational abilities.

5.1 Pragmatics and Discourse Analysis during Clinical Interactions

Much of the communication in clinical settings is varied and sometimes controlled and artificial, meaning it doesn't mirror real-life communication experiences but rather revolves around the targets for example of a medical assessment or a specific language therapy. An option that has recently gained attention to address this unnatural setting for communication in healthcare practice is to advocate for a sociolinguistic approach to analysing pragmatic communication. This approach considers the influence of personal and environmental factors on communication in clinical settings (Keegan et al., 2023). It is aligned with the International Classification of Functioning, Disability and Health (ICF) model developed by the World Health Organization (WHO, 2001), as discussed in Section 1.

Individuals with **social (pragmatic) communication disorder** (SPCD), as well as individuals with other communication disorders, exhibit significant heterogeneity. Consequently, assessing communication difficulties often relies on unpredictable factors and individual experiences heavily influenced by context and environment. Achieving a clinical assessment that is both valid and reliable amid such complexity is challenging. Many times, impairment-based tests, or 'standardised tests,' fall short in capturing communication abilities and disregard contextual factors crucial to pragmatic communication. Assessing single impairment cognitive/language skills, such as memory, attention, or language comprehension, fails to provide insights into pragmatic abilities in patients with SPCD. These assessments overlook environmental influences, interaction demands, and personal characteristics brought into conversations by individuals. Conversations serve as optimal units of investigation in SPCD, with their analyses requiring minimal theoretical knowledge of modulating factors. In clinical settings, decisions regarding discourse sampling involve considering various factors. For instance, if examining a core linguistic function, such as semantics or syntax, a monologic discourse sampling like narrative retelling or picture description may be suitable. However, for assessing conversational abilities, contexts such as interviews or specific conversational settings should be integrated with normative assessments to better elicit pragmatic skills, such as the use of Speech acts, the coherence and the informativeness of an answer.

Clinical tools emerging from this approach are increasingly utilised. For instance, analysing requests/provisions of information or actions within an exchange analysis framework reveals challenges faced by individuals with SPCD, such as misinterpretation or lack of interaction. Dynamic moves in a conversation, like introducing new meanings or negotiating mutual understanding through clarifications or feedback, are common in discourse studies. Moreover, employing dynamic moves can create challenging conversational contexts by soliciting justifications or critical opinions. This conversational skills-based approach allows clinicians to identify individuals' roles in conversational contexts and understand how they and their communication partners contribute to interactions. Additionally, contextual descriptions enable exploration of the patient–professional relationship and how it evolves through semantic selections during interpersonal communication. It is also essential to acknowledge that nurses or doctors may adopt different conversational approaches based on their roles and relationships with patients.

In addition to the dynamic move analyses presented previously where the focus is on meaning and ideas (see also Biber et al., 2007 for more details), topic analysis proves relevant for focusing on patterns in topic management that are either accessible or require attention due to communication difficulties. Topic analysis involves investigating factors such as how topics are introduced, the coherence of topic changes, the sustainability of topics, and the core disruptions on specific topics (Bedrosian, 1993). Transitivity analysis, which examines how speakers portray themselves in relation to the world they interact with, is another valuable tool during conversations. It allows for the examination of how individuals construe and present their experiences (Keegan & Müller, 2022; Keegan et al., 2022). This analysis classifies verbs used as material, behavioural, mental, relational, or existential, providing insight into how speakers develop propositional attitudes from their perspectives, thereby informing clinicians about their cognitive abilities. Appraisal analysis is another aspect that can be tracked to understand how individuals express their opinions and perspectives, facilitating direct interaction with speakers (Keegan & Müller, 2022). For instance, it examines quantification of information (e.g., 'much better', 'much worse') or direct evaluations of people's feelings, as well as their level of engagement with the interlocutor.

Modality analysis is another intriguing investigation of discourse in healthcare settings. It involves examining discourse that is not explicitly polarised but rather based on undefined areas of meaning, addressing potentiality and probability in conversation. This high-level analysis can be applied, for example, in tracking humour, politeness markers, and intentions (Keegan et al., 2021; Meulenbroek & Cherney, 2021).

In addition to the aforementioned aspects, collecting a representative conversational sample necessitates thorough training regarding expectations and approach. This includes deciding whether to record audio or video conversations, especially if analysis of non-verbal communication is relevant. Another crucial factor is the contribution of communication partners to the interactions. Ideally, conversations should feature a balanced set of opportunities for both parties to engage. However, this conversation equity can be disrupted by social pragmatic communication disorder (SPCD), leading to issues such as poor turn-taking, verbosity, difficulty generating topics, and impaired judgement regarding the social situation.

The development of communication training programmes for carers, such as families and friends (Rietdijk et al., 2020; Togher et al., 2016), has advanced outcome measure development. This includes the use of rating scales to assess the interactional/transitional skills of individuals with traumatic brain injury (TBI) and the conversational support strategies used by their partners (Togher et al., 2010). Recent expansions in sociolinguistic analysis have seen examination of the communication characteristics of participants with TBI interacting not only in dyads but also in group settings. Best practice guidelines recommend using group treatment where possible for communication disability following TBI (Togher et al., 2014), necessitating the development of new tools to examine group interaction dynamics. Communication partners play a significant role in interactions involving individuals with communication difficulties. Factors such as interlocutor relationships, power dynamics, training, culture, and identity all influence the dynamics of interactions and should be considered when examining communication within the context of an individual's partners.

One criticism of implementing the **sociolinguistic model** in clinical settings has been the trade-off between time and data collection. However, advancements in discourse-related technologies now offer more opportunities for implementing a sociolinguistic model of pragmatic communication without the need for transcription of data. For example, the Interactional Network Tool (INT; Howell et al., 2021) is an electronic analysis tool that qualifies and quantifies interactions between communication partners in group settings based on video data analysis. Further exploration of AI and pragmatics will be discussed in Section 5.3.

5.2 The Use of Metaphors in Health Communication

A widely investigated pragmatic tool in healthcare practice is the use of metaphors in interactions between clinicians and patients, and in health communication in general (see also Section 4.4). Metaphors play a vital role in healthcare communication (Casarett et al., 2010; Landau et al., 2018). Various areas of healthcare, such as oncology and mental health, have developed specific uses of metaphors that are regularly incorporated into practice, therapy, and conversations among healthcare providers, patients, and their relatives (Littlemore & Turner, 2019; Malkomsen et al., 2022; Semino et al., 2017).

As introduced in the previous section, modern-day research on metaphors in healthcare surged with the publication of *Metaphors We Live By* by linguists Lakoff and Johnson (1980). Their conceptual metaphor theory posits that metaphors are more than mere decorative figures of speech; rather, they have a profound impact on our perceptions, thoughts, and subsequent actions. Metaphoric language is commonplace in psychotherapy, where there is a need to convey or retain a sense of ambiguity when describing phenomena like the 'black cloud' of depression. In such cases, metaphors serve as bridges between familiar, tangible concepts (the metaphor vehicle) and abstract descriptions of phenomena. A metaphor involves comparing two entities, implying similarities between them. Metaphors generate mental images that encapsulate clusters of information, facilitating faster comprehension as they navigate the brain.

Metaphors have been reported to have a supportive effect on communication in healthcare from both doctors' and patients' perspectives, and they are integrated into healthcare training (Spina et al., 2018). Metaphors prove particularly useful in situations where there is an imbalance in language proficiency, such as when a doctor and a patient do not share the same dominant language (first language, L1) or if they are both second language (L2) speakers. Metaphorical language serves as a deliberate mechanism to compensate for the lack of specific term knowledge and to adopt a richer propositional attitude in describing complex facts. As metaphorical competence appears to develop alongside other language skills (Littlemore, 2019), it is pertinent to facilitate its development, especially for second-language doctors and other professions requiring refined communication skills. There is a growing need for training on metaphorical language in healthcare, considering the linguistic backgrounds of both speakers.

Another well-studied aspect of metaphorical language in healthcare literature is the semantic concepts associated with metaphors (Semino, 2021). For instance, whether expressions encourage an active approach to how the listener should respond to the metaphor. For example, in a quote from the Prime Minister of the United Kingdom during the Covid-19 pandemic, it is evident that the speaker aims to establish common ground for the conversation and utilise the context of war metaphors to deliver a powerful and resolute message.

> Yes this enemy can be deadly, but it is also beatable – and we know how to beat it and we know that if as a country we follow the scientific advice that is now being given we know that we will beat it. And however tough the months ahead we have the resolve and the resources to win the fight.
>
> (Boris Johnson, UK Prime Minister, 17 March 2020)

War metaphors in the medical context have been subject to study, revealing a potentially counterproductive framing effect, particularly in oncology and cancer prevention contexts. Research indicates that war metaphors can increase fatalism among cancer patients and reduce individuals' willingness to engage in preventive measures, such as smoking cessation or alcohol reduction (Hauser & Schwarz, 2020).

Further studies on the use of war metaphors in oncology have highlighted their association with increased attribution of guilt to patients who fail to recover from cancer, thereby hindering the promotion of positive preventive behaviours (Hendricks et al., 2018). Interestingly, alternative semantic frameworks, such as journey metaphors, have been identified as more effective and less likely to foster a 'fighter' representation in individuals facing illness (Hendricks et al., 2018).

Metaphors are potent communication tools necessary for effective communication, yet they can also lead to misinterpretation, especially in conditions that are challenging to describe (see Bullo, 2020, for a study on the communication challenges of endometriosis pain). An integrated approach involving linguists, healthcare professionals, and patients could yield a comprehensive set of tools where various metaphors can be matched to different types of pain, facilitating visual communication and gestures. Such an approach, already proven effective in oncology (Semino et al., 2017), would enable more nuanced discussions, particularly regarding symptoms in early consultations. Moreover, it could be incorporated into educational programmes to enhance communication practices and language efficacy.

5.3 Pragmatics-AI for Mental Healthcare

Recent advancements in communication technologies present a significant opportunity to promote and investigate the pragmatic abilities of speakers. As previously discussed, a single assessment measure may not adequately capture all aspects of social communication. To obtain a more comprehensive sample during a conversation, a variety of contextual communication interactions must be observed. One promising avenue is the incorporation of artificial intelligence (AI) conversation tools, which offer several advantages, including reduced emotional demands, streamlined data collection processes, and the ability to provide consistent, repeatable interactions.

Several potential applications of AI in pragmatic language assessment and intervention have emerged in recent literature. Advanced conversation analysis tools powered by AI can analyse conversations in real time, identifying pragmatic features such as turn-taking, topic maintenance, and use of context-appropriate language. For example, the work-related communication training approach (WoRC) utilises a computer-based role-play treatment to engage users in practising strategic politeness markers commonly encountered in workplace environments (Meulenbroek & Cherney, 2021). In individuals with pragmatic disorders, politeness markers expressed in language (e.g., should, could, would) are often underused despite being contextually required. WoRC software employs speech-to-text technology to transcribe and score users' use of politeness markers, providing tailored feedback. The software's flexibility allows it to record and adapt to individual needs, supporting interaction observation without requiring full transcription. Various tools, such as the Pragmatic Rating Scale (Iwashita & Sohlberg, 2019), supplement this approach by allowing clinicians to rate interactions in real time using a checklist-style format.

AI-driven conversational agents, like Woebot, offer platforms for practising conversational turns and social interactions in a low-pressure environment, indirectly supporting pragmatic language skills. In addition to its applications in language practice, Woebot has been successfully utilised to help individuals manage depression, demonstrating its versatility and effectiveness in mental health interventions (Fitzpatrick et al., 2017). Virtual reality (VR) systems, such as VIRTUOSO, provide realistic social scenarios for autistic individuals to practise pragmatic language use and receive feedback in a controlled setting. VR environments can be customised to simulate a wide range of social situations, from casual conversations to more complex interactions like job interviews or group discussions (Schmidt et al., 2019). Additionally, social robots like Milo from RoboKind (2020) interact with children using consistent speech patterns, aiding in the development of social communication skills.

These robots can also be particularly beneficial for autistic children, as they provide predictable, non-judgemental interactions that can help build confidence in social communication. Finally, wearable devices equipped with AI, such as those incorporating Brain Power software for Google Glass, have shown promise in improving social communication skills in autistic children by enhancing factors such as facial engagement and emotion recognition (Melo et al., 2019; Voss et al., 2019). These interventions suggest a potential role for Pragmatic-AI in enhancing social communication and may contribute to the improvement of autism behavioural therapy, which is often costly and challenging to access. Mobile-based technology therapy has the potential to mitigate logistical challenges and scale to meet increasing demand from autistic patients.

Currently, less than 10 per cent of speech-language pathologists routinely assess social communication, despite its significant impact on **quality of life**, professional outcomes, and personal relationships (Frith et al., 2014). This statistic underscores the need for more accessible and efficient assessment tools. Most assessments still rely on traditional impairment-based measures, although pragmatic rating scales are widely used. These scales should be complemented with the conversation sampling process described previously. However, due to a lack of agreement on comparable and repeatable sample techniques, there are presently no guidelines for clinicians. New communication rating systems, when paired with sampling processes and aided by trained technologies, may offer a partial solution to this challenge. Recently, AI has further been employed to create tests for pragmatic competencies in second language learning, with procedural methods necessary to ensure the tool's authenticity (O'Grady, 2023). This application demonstrates the potential for AI to support pragmatic language development across diverse populations and contexts.

In conclusion, the intersection of AI and pragmatic language assessment and intervention represents an exciting frontier in speech and language therapy. By leveraging these technologies thoughtfully and in conjunction with established clinical practices, we have the potential to significantly enhance our ability to support individuals with pragmatic language difficulties, ultimately improving their social communication skills, quality of life, and overall well-being. Future research should focus on validating these AI tools across diverse populations, integrating them effectively into clinical practice, and exploring their long-term impact on pragmatic language outcomes. Additionally, ethical considerations, such as data privacy and the potential for over-reliance on technology, must be carefully addressed as these tools become more prevalent.

5.4 Intercultural Pragmatics and the Problem of Health Inequalities

Pragmatic communication skills are significantly influenced by an individual's cultural background. Linguist Gary Prideaux formally recognised the potential contribution of cultural influences on pragmatic abilities (1991), proposing that some pragmatic principles, such as those proposed by Grice, are rooted in social conventions of the culture – termed social pragmatic principles. On the other hand, linguistic pragmatic principles arise from human capacities in language processing and are consistent across cultures due to being cognitively determined, rather than culturally specific.

This framework, distinguishing between social and linguistic pragmatic principles, holds heuristic and clinical value. Heuristically, it aids in framing pragmatics as encompassing two distinct yet interconnected domains – social and linguistic – as discussed in Section 1. This approach can effectively resolve issues such as categorising various behaviours, including manners and confabulation, under the umbrella of 'pragmatic behaviours'. It also helps understand how specific behaviours, such as turn-taking, can be influenced by both cultural and cognitive factors.

From a clinical perspective, the framework suggests a direction for assessing pragmatic ability, recommending the consideration and evaluation of both linguistic and social aspects. These aspects are often dissociable in many clinical populations, as demonstrated in case studies. For instance, children with reported intellectual disabilities may exhibit better proficiency in certain pragmatic communication functions, such as politeness, compared to what their language skills would predict. Conversely, populations such as autistic children may demonstrate pragmatic communication impairments disproportionate to their language skill levels.

Furthermore, this framework aids in distinguishing behaviours related to factors like culture and socioeconomic status from those attributable to neuropsychological deficits, crucial for evaluating social behaviour in culturally diverse populations. Consequently, cultural factors should be considered in diagnosing pragmatic disorders.

Studies on bilingual adults with ADHD, for instance, have shown differing profiles in pragmatic disorder symptoms between their first and second languages, highlighting the influence of linguistic factors (Köder et al., 2024a; Köder et al., 2024b). There is a worldwide risk that people with an immigration background tend to be at risk of being under-diagnosed for ADHD (Hansen et al. 2023), due to multiple factors, from genetic predisposition to knowledge of the healthcare system or language-related factors. An adult at risk of ADHD with an immigration background might get assessed and interviewed in the language dominant in the community, which might not be the first language. This can have a huge impact on the validity of the clinical assessment, with communicative symptoms of hyperactivity and impulsivity such as interrupting people reported as most strongly pronounced in a person's first language. Conducting diagnostic interviews and tests in a person's second or third language might therefore potentially mask communicative hyperactivity and impulsivity symptoms, increasing the risk of underdiagnosing ADHD in multilingual speakers who are not evaluated in their dominant language.

Addressing the emergent global issue of **health inequalities** due to neglecting cultural aspects is crucial. Healthcare services must cater to the diverse needs of linguistically and culturally diverse service users to reduce diagnostic overshadowing. Health inequalities, including difficulties in identifying diseases on patients with darker skin tones, particularly affect minority groups. Racism is identified as an equitable healthcare barrier, exacerbating health disparities (Hamed et al., 2022). Thus, calls for decolonisation of healthcare curriculums and standardised testing have arisen to reduce these inequalities.

A more holistic approach, incorporating pragmatics factors discussed in this section, is recommended in healthcare. Viewing hospitals as cultural institutions of healthcare within a region and clinicians as intermediaries between culture/environment and patient situations allows for investigation of the healthcare context as a cultural phenomenon. This approach aligns with proposed Integrated Care Systems focusing on places and local populations as drivers for health improvement.

Conclusions

In this Element, we have embarked on an exploration of pragmatics as it intersects with health sciences. Our journey has traversed diverse territories, including clinical pragmatics, experimental pragmatics, cognitive aspects of communication disorders, and the application of pragmatic principles in health practice. However, it is imperative to acknowledge that the breadth of pragmatics extends far beyond what we could comprehensively cover in this introductory volume. The field is expansive, dynamic, and continually evolving, encompassing diverse perspectives and integrating the new frontiers of medical AI.

Pragmatics, within the realm of medical humanities, keeps illuminating critical aspects of healthcare communication, patient narratives, and the ethical dimensions of medical practice. It offers a lens to analyse how language choices, communicative strategies, and cultural factors shape interactions between patients and healthcare providers (Charon, 2006; Hamilton & Chou, 2014). By examining linguistic features such as politeness, empathy, and indirectness, pragmatics enhances our understanding of patient-centred care, shared decision-making, and the construction of illness narratives. For instance, research showed how doctors' discourse styles significantly impact patient satisfaction and treatment adherence. Physicians who adopt a socio-relational framework, rather than a purely biomedical one, listen attentively to what the patient says, use the patient's own life experiences to build the discourse, and respect the patient as a whole person. This deep empathy approach, as defined by Topol in his seminal work (Topol, 2023), fosters a sense of being heard, understood, and cared for, encouraging patients to share personal and sometimes difficult stories, which can enhance medical outcomes. Conversely, the absence of friendliness and warmth, failure to meet patient expectations, and use of confusing terminology and instructions contribute to patient dissatisfaction (Cordella, 2004).

Furthermore, pragmatic frameworks aid in addressing ethical dilemmas in medical communication and developing culturally competent healthcare practices. The study of doctor–patient interactions increasingly focuses on how patients' ethnic backgrounds influence medical communication, particularly as health practitioners encounter more culturally diverse patients. Intercultural consultations often involve more misunderstandings and lower satisfaction compared to intra-cultural ones. Ethnic minority patients tend to be less expressive, and providers often find these interactions more challenging. Additionally, disparities in healthcare access and outcomes exist, partly due to communication gaps (for a review, Schouten & Meeuwesen, 2006). Pragmatics also entered psychotherapy, where linguistic elements such as proverbs, metaphors, and idioms play crucial roles. Pragmatic analysis can reveal subtle communication patterns that influence therapeutic outcomes (a.o., Chaika, 2008; Ephratt, 2014; Lepper, 2009).

Finally, we should consider how digital health communication offers vast potential but also presents unique challenges. For example, the asynchronous nature of many online health forums can lead to unique pragmatic challenges, such as maintaining coherence across extended discussions or interpreting emotion and intention without non-verbal cues (Yu, 2011). Additionally, social media health communication fosters quick information sharing and interactive participation, but it also presents difficulties including the propagation of false information and privacy issues, requiring careful management and well-thought -out messages (for a recent review, see Afful-Dadzie et al., 2023). Furthermore, automated dialogue systems that can mimic in-person interactions between healthcare providers and patients are being made possible by emerging technologies like artificial intelligence (AI) and natural language processing (NLP). For example, consider the growing popularity of mobile and home-based conversational assistants. But if not done right, these patient-facing conversational interfaces can potentially provide serious hazards (Bickmore et al., 2018).

To sum up, this Element has established the foundation for comprehending the critical function of pragmatics in the health sciences. As time goes on, it becomes evident that solving the complex communication problems in healthcare would require ongoing study and the implementation of practical ideas. Pragmatics provides a useful lens through which we may comprehend and enhance health outcomes, from bettering doctor–patient communication to boosting the efficacy of digital health treatments. This volume marks the beginning of a long and hopeful route towards more efficient, compassionate, and culturally aware healthcare communication.

References

Ackerman, B. P. (1983). Form and function in children's understanding of ironic utterances. *Journal of Experimental Child Psychology, 35*(3), 487–508. https://doi.org/10.1016/0022-0965(83)90023-1.

Adesope, O. O., Lavin, T., Thompson, T., & Ungerleider, C. (2010). A systematic review and meta-analysis of the cognitive correlates of bilingualism. *Review of Educational Research, 80*(2), 207–245. https://doi.org/10.3102/00346543 103688.

Adornetti, I., Chiera, A., Altavilla, D. et al. (2021). Self-projection in middle childhood: A study on the relationship between theory of mind and episodic future thinking. *Cognitive Processing, 22*, 321–332. https://doi.org/10.1007/ s10339-021-01013-w.

Afful-Dadzie, E., Afful-Dadzie, A., & Egala, S. B. (2023). Social media in health communication: A literature review of information quality. *Health Information Management Journal, 52*(1), 3–17. https://doi.org/10.1177/183335832 1992683.

Amanzio, M., Geminiani, G., Leotta, D., & Cappa, S. (2008). Metaphor comprehension in Alzheimer's disease: Novelty matters. *Brain and Language, 107*(1), 1–10. https://doi.org/10.1016/j.bandl.2007.08.003.

American Psychiatric Association (APA), DSM-5 Task Force. (2013). *Diagnostic and Statistical Manual of Mental Disorders: DSM-5 (5th ed.).* Arlington: American Psychiatric Association. https://doi.org/10.1176/appi .books.9780890425596.

American Psychiatric Association. (2022). *Diagnostic and Statistical Manual of Mental Disorders* (5th ed., text rev.). Arlington: American Psychiatric Association. https://doi.org/10.1176/appi.books.9780890425787.

Anderson, K. K., Khan, J. A., Edwards, J. et al. (2024). Lost in translation? Deciphering the role of language differences in the excess risk of psychosis among migrant groups. *Psychological Medicine, 54*(11), 3063–3070. https://doi .org/10.1017/S003329172400117X.

Andrés-Roqueta, C., & Katsos, N. (2020). A distinction between linguistic and social pragmatics helps the precise characterization of pragmatic challenges in children with autism spectrum disorders and developmental language disorder. *Journal of Speech, Language, and Hearing Research, 63*(5), 1494–1508.

Angeleri, R., Bosco, F. M., Zettin, M., Sacco, K., Colle, L., & Bara, B. G. (2008). Communicative impairment in traumatic brain injury: A complete pragmatic assessment. *Brain and Language, 107*(3), 229–245. https://doi.org/10.1016/j.bandl.2008.01.002.

Angeleri, R., Gabbatore, I., Bosco, F. M., Sacco, K., & Colle, L. (2016). Pragmatic abilities in children and adolescents with autism spectrum disorder: A study with the ABaCo battery. *Minerva Psichiatrica, 57*(3), 93–103. https://api.semanticscholar.org/CorpusID:150287927.

Arcara, G., & Bambini, V. (2016). A test for the Assessment of Pragmatic Abilities and Cognitive Substrates (APACS): Normative data and psychometric properties. *Frontiers in Psychology, 7*, 1–13. https://doi.org/10.3389/fpsyg.2016.00070.

Arrondo, G., Sepulcre, J., Duque, B., Toledo, J., & Villoslada, P. (2010). Narrative speech is impaired in multiple sclerosis. *The European Neurological Journal, 2*(1), 11–40.

Arvidsson, C., Pagmar, D., & Uddén, J. (2022). When did you stop speaking to yourself? Age-related differences in adolescents' world knowledge-based audience design. *Royal Society Open Science, 9*(11), 1–14. https://doi.org/10.1098/rsos.220305.

Asaridou, S. S., Demir-Lira, Ö. E., Uddén, J., Goldin-Meadow, S., & Small, S. L. (2019). Pragmatic language processing in the adolescent brain. *BioRxiv*, 871343. https://doi.org/10.1101/871343.

Austin, J. L. (1975). *How to Do Things with Words*. Cambridge: Harvard University Press.

Bambini, V., Arcara, G., Martinelli, I. et al. (2016). Communication and pragmatic breakdowns in amyotrophic lateral sclerosis patients. *Brain and Language, 153*, 1–12. https://doi.org/10.1016/j.bandl.2015.12.002.

Bambini, V., Bischetti, L., Bonomi, C. G. et al. (2020a). Beyond the motor account of amyotrophic lateral sclerosis: Verbal humour and its relationship with the cognitive and pragmatic profile. *International Journal of Language & Communication Disorders, 55*(5), 751–764. https://doi.org/10.1111/1460-6984.12561.

Bambini, V., Gentili, C., Ricciardi, E., Bertinetto, P. M., & Pietrini, P. (2011). Decomposing metaphor processing at the cognitive and neural level through functional magnetic resonance imaging. *Brain Research Bulletin, 86*(3–4), 203–216. https://doi.org/10.1016/j.brainresbull.2011.07.015.

Bambini, V., Van Looy, L., Demiddele, K., & Schaeken, W. (2021). What is the contribution of executive functions to communicative-pragmatic skills? Insights from aging and different types of pragmatic inference. *Cognitive Processing, 22*(3), 435–452. https://doi.org/10.1007/s10339-021-01021-w.

Bambini, V., Tonini, E., Ceccato, I. et al. (2020b). How to improve social communication in aging: Pragmatic and cognitive interventions. *Brain and Language*, *211*, 1–13. https://doi.org/10.1016/j.bandl.2020.104864.

Banasik, N., & Podsiadło, K. (2016). Comprehension of ironic utterances by bilingual children. *Psychology of Language and Communication*, *20*(3), 316–335. https://doi.org/10.1515/plc-2016-0019.

Barnett, M. D., Smith, L. N., Sandlin, A. M., & Coldiron, A. M. (2023). Loneliness and off-topic verbosity among young adults and older adults. *Psychological Reports*, *126*(2), 641–655. https://doi.org/10.1177/00332941211058045.

Baron-Cohen, S., Leslie, A. M., & Frith, U. (1985). Does the autistic child have a 'theory of mind'? *Cognition*, *21*(1), 37–46. https://doi.org/10.1016/0010-0277(85)90022-8.

Bates, E., Camaioni, L., & Volterra, V. (1975). The acquisition of performatives prior to speech. *Merrill-Palmer Quarterly of Behavior and Development*, *21* (3), 205–226. www.jstor.org/stable/23084619.

Bedrosian, J. L. (1993). Making minds meet: Assessment of conversational topic in adults with mild to moderate mental retardation. *Topics in Language Disorders*, *13*(3), 36–46. https://doi.org/10.1097/00011363-199305000-00006.

Bernstein, D. M., Thornton, W. L., & Sommerville, J. A. (2011). Theory of mind through the ages: Older and middle-aged adults exhibit more errors than do younger adults on a continuous false belief task. *Experimental Aging Research*, *37*(5), 481–502. https://doi.org/10.1080/0361073X.2011.619466.

Biber, D., Connor, U. & Upton, T. A. (2007). *Discourse on the Move: Studies in Corpus Linguistics, 28*, Amsterdam: John Benjamins, p. 289.

Bickmore, T., Trinh, H., Asadi, R., & Olafsson, S. (2018). Safety first: Conversational agents for health care. In Moore, R., Szymanski, M., Arar, R., & Ren, G. J. (Eds.), *Studies in Conversational UX Design: Human–Computer Interaction Series*, Cham: Springer, pp. 33–57. https://doi.org/10.1007/978-3-319-95579-7_3.

Bischetti, L., Ceccato, I., Lecce, S., Cavallini, E., & Bambini, V. (2023). Pragmatics and theory of mind in older adults' humor comprehension. *Current Psychology*, *42*(19), 16191–16207. https://doi.org/10.1007/s12144-019-00295-w.

Bischetti, L., Frau, F., & Bambini, V. (2024). Neuropragmatics. In Ball, M. J., Müller, N., & Spencer, L. (Eds.), *Handbook of Clinical Linguistics* (*2nd ed.*), Hoboken: Wiley Blackwell, pp. 41–54.

Bishop, D. V. (2006). *Children's communication checklist – 2nd ed.: CCC-2*. San Antonio: Harcourt Assessment.

Bishop, D. V. (2014). Pragmatic language impairment: A correlate of SLI, a distinct subgroup, or part of the autistic continuum? In Bishop, D. V., & Leonard, L. B. (Eds.), *Speech and Language Impairments in Children: Causes, Characteristics, Intervention and Outcome*, Philadelphia: Psychology Press, pp. 99–113.

Bitsko, R. H., Claussen, A. H., Lichstein, J. et al. (2022). Mental health surveillance among children – United States, 2013–2019. *MMWR Supplements, 71* (2), 1–42.

Bohn, M., & Frank, M. C. (2019). The pervasive role of pragmatics in early language. *Annual Review of Developmental Psychology, 1*, 223–249. https://doi.org/10.1146/annurev-devpsych-121318-085037.

Bohn, M., Tessler, M. H., Kordt, C., Hausmann, T., & Frank, M. C. (2023). An individual differences perspective on pragmatic abilities in the preschool years. *Developmental Science, 26*, e13401. https://doi.org/10.1111/desc.13401.

Bosco, F. M., Angeleri, R., Sacco, K., & Bara, B. G. (2015). Explaining pragmatic performance in traumatic brain injury: A process perspective on communicative errors. *International Journal of Language & Communication Disorders, 50*(1), 63–83. https://doi.org/10.1111/1460-6984.12114.

Bosco, F. M., Angeleri, R., Zuffranieri, M., Bara, B. G., & Sacco, K. (2012). Assessment battery for communication: Development of two equivalent forms. *Journal of Communication Disorders, 45*(4), 290–303. https://doi.org/10.1016/j.jcomdis.2012.03.002.

Bosco, F. M., & Bucciarelli, M. (2008). Simple and complex deceits and ironies. *Journal of Pragmatics, 40*(4), 583–607. https://doi.org/10.1016/j.pragma.2007.05.004.

Bosco, F. M., Gabbatore, I., & Tirassa, M. (2014). A broad assessment of theory of mind in adolescence: The complexity of mindreading. *Consciousness and Cognition, 24*, 84–97. https://doi.org/10.1016/j.concog.2014.01.003.

Bott, L., & Noveck, I. A. (2004). Some utterances are underinformative: The onset and time course of scalar inferences. *Journal of Memory and Language, 51*(3), 437–457. https://doi.org/10.1016/j.jml.2004.05.006.

Bromberek-Dyzman, K., & Rataj, K. (2016). Irony comprehension in the nonnative language comes at a cost. *Psychology of Language and Communication, 20*(3), 336–353. https://doi.org/10.1515/plc-2016-0020.

Bruner, J. S. (1975). The ontogenesis of speech acts. *Journal of Child Language, 2*(1), 1–19. https://doi.org/10.1017/S0305000900000866.

Bullo, S. (2020). 'I feel like I'm being stabbed by a thousand tiny men': The challenges of communicating endometriosis pain. *Health, 24*(5), 476–492. https://doi.org/10.1177/1363459318817943.

Campanha, A. C., Lira, J. O., Diniz, A. et al. (2008). IC-P1-007: Performance comparison of Alzheimer disease and healthy subjects in interpretation of popular proverbs. *Alzheimer's & Dementia*, 4(4S_Part_1), T12–T12. https://doi.org/10.1016/j.jalz.2008.05.020.

Canali, S., Altavilla, D., Acciai, A. et al. (2021). The narrative of persons with gambling problems and substance use: A multidimensional analysis of the language of addiction. *Journal of Gambling Issues*, 47, 7, 167–198. https://doi.org/10.4309/jgi.2021.47.7.

Cardillo, R., Mammarella, I. C., Demurie, E., Giofre, D., & Roeyers, H. (2021). Pragmatic language in children and adolescents with autism spectrum disorder: Do theory of mind and executive functions have a mediating role?. *Autism Research*, 14(5), 932–945. https://doi.org/10.1002/aur.2423.

Carotenuto, A., Arcara, G., Orefice, G. et al. (2018a). Communication in multiple sclerosis: Pragmatic deficit and its relation with cognition and social cognition. *Archives of Clinical Neuropsychology*, 33(2), 194–205. https://doi.org/10.1093/arclin/acx061.

Carotenuto, A., Cocozza, S., Quarantelli, M. et al. (2018b). Pragmatic abilities in multiple sclerosis: The contribution of the temporo-parietal junction. *Brain and Language*, 185, 47–53. https://doi.org/10.1016/j.bandl.2018.08.003.

Carpenter, M., Nagell, K., Tomasello, M., Butterworth, G., & Moore, C. (1998). Social cognition, joint attention, and communicative competence from 9 to 15 months of age. *Monographs of the Society for Research in Child Development*, 63(4), 1–143. https://doi.org/10.2307/1166214.

Carruthers, S., Taylor, L., Sadiq, H., & Tripp, G. (2022). The profile of pragmatic language impairments in children with ADHD: A systematic review. *Development and Psychopathology*, 34(5), 1938–1960. https://doi.org/10.1017/S0954579421000328.

Casarett, D., Pickard, A., Fishman, J. M. et al. (2010). Can metaphors and analogies improve communication with seriously ill patients? *Journal of Palliative Medicine*, 13(3), 255–260. https://doi.org/10.1089/jpm.2009.0221.

Cavell, T. A. (1990). Social adjustment, social performance, and social skills: A tri-component model of social competence. *Journal of Clinical Child Psychology*, 19(2), 111–122. https://doi.org/10.1207/s15374424jccp1902_2.

Chaika, E. (2008). *Linguistics, Pragmatics and Psychotherapy: A Guide for Therapists*. Hoboken: Wiley Blackwell .

Chakrabarty, M., Klooster, N., Biswas, A., & Chatterjee, A. (2023). The scope of using pragmatic language tests for early detection of dementia: A systematic review of investigations using figurative language. *Alzheimer's & Dementia: The Journal of the Alzheimer's Association*, 19(10), 4705–4728. https://doi.org/10.1002/alz.13369.

Charon, R. (2006). *Narrative Medicine*: *Honoring the Stories of Illness*. Oxford: Oxford University Press.

Chemla, E., & Singh, R. (2014). Remarks on the experimental turn in the study of scalar implicature, Part II. *Language and Linguistics Compass*, *8*(9), 387–399. https://doi.org/10.1111/lnc3.12080.

Chomsky, N. (1959). A review of BF Skinner's verbal behavior. *Language*, *35*(1), 26–58. www.jstor.org/stable/i217081.

Colle, L., Angeleri, R., Vallana, M. et al. (2013). Understanding the communicative impairments in schizophrenia: A preliminary study. *Journal of Communication Disorders*, *46*(3), 294–308. https://doi.org/10.1016/j.jcomdis.2013.01.003.

Cordella, M. (2004). *The Dynamic Consultation*: *A Discourse Analytical Study of Doctor–Patient Communication*. Amsterdam: John Benjamins.

Costa, A., Hernández, M., & Sebastián-Gallés, N. (2008). Bilingualism aids conflict resolution: Evidence from the ANT task. *Cognition*, *106*(1), 59–86. https://doi.org/10.1016/j.cognition.2006.12.013.

Craik, F. I., & Bialystok, E. (2006). Cognition through the lifespan: Mechanisms of change. *Trends in Cognitive Sciences*, *10*(3), 131–138. https://doi.org/10.1016/j.tics.2006.01.007.

Crone, E. A., & Dahl, R. E. (2012). Understanding adolescence as a period of social – affective engagement and goal flexibility. *Nature Reviews Neuroscience*, *13*(9), 636–650. https://doi.org/10.1038/nrn3313.

Cummings, L. (2009). *Clinical Pragmatics*. Cambridge: Cambridge University Press.

Cummings, L. (2017). Cognitive aspects of pragmatic disorders. In Cummings, L. (Eds.), *Research in Clinical Pragmatics*: *Perspectives in Pragmatics, Philosophy & Psychology, vol 11*. Cham: Springer, pp. 587–616. https://doi.org/10.1007/978-3-319-47489-2_22.

Cummings, L. (2021). *Handbook of Pragmatic Language Disorders: Complex and Underserved Populations*. Cham: Springer.

Cutica, I., Bucciarelli, M., & Bara, B. G. (2006). Neuropragmatics: Extralinguistic pragmatic ability is better preserved in left-hemisphere-damaged patients than in right-hemisphere-damaged patients. *Brain and Language*, *98*(1), 12–25. https://doi.org/10.1016/j.bandl.2006.01.001.

Davis, B. H., Guendouzi, J., & Morón, R. G. (Eds.). (2014). *Pragmatics in Dementia Discourse*. Newcastle upon Tyne: Cambridge Scholars.

DESA, UN Department for Economic and Social Affairs (2023). www.un.org/development/desa/dspd/wp-content/uploads/sites/22/2023/01/WSR_2023_Chapter_Key_Messages.pdf.

Domaneschi, F., & Di Paola, S. (2019). The ageing factor in presupposition processing. *Journal of Pragmatics*, *140*, 70–87. https://doi.org/10.1016/j.pragma.2018.11.014.

Duncan, H. D., Nikelski, J., Pilon, R. et al. (2018). Structural brain differences between monolingual and multilingual patients with mild cognitive impairment and Alzheimer disease: Evidence for cognitive reserve. *Neuropsychologia, 109*, 270–282. https://doi.org/10.1016/j.neuropsychologia.2017.12.036.

Ephratt, M. (2014). Grice's cooperative principle in the psychoanalytic setting. *The Psychoanalytic Review, 101*(6), 815–845. https://doi.org/10.1521/prev.2014.101.6.815.

Fägersten, K. B. (2012). *Who's Swearing Now? The Social Aspects of Conversational Swearing*. Newcastle upon Tyne: Cambridge Scholars.

Fairchild, S., & Papafragou, A. (2018). Sins of omission are more likely to be forgiven in non-native speakers. *Cognition, 181*, 80–92. https://doi.org/10.1016/j.cognition.2018.08.010.

Falkum, I. L., & Köder, F. (2020). The acquisition of figurative meanings. *Journal of Pragmatics, 164*, 18–24. https://doi.org/10.1016/j.pragma.2020.04.007.

Ferstl, E. C., & von Cramon, D. Y. (2001). The role of coherence and cohesion in text comprehension: An event-related fMRI study. *Cognitive Brain Research, 11*(3), 325–340. https://doi.org/10.1016/S0926-6410(01)00007-6.

Filippova, E. (2014). Irony production and comprehension. In Matthews, D. (Ed.), *Pragmatic Development in First Language Acquisition*, Amsterdam: John Benjamins, pp. 261–278. https://doi.org/10.1075/tilar.10.15fil.

Fitzpatrick, K. K., Darcy, A., & Vierhile, M. (2017). Delivering cognitive behavior therapy to young adults with symptoms of depression and anxiety using a fully automated conversational agent (Woebot): A randomized controlled trial. *JMIR Mental Health, 4*(2), e7785. https://doi.org.10.2196/mental.7785.

Foppolo, F., & Mazzaggio, G. (2024). 2 Conversational implicature and communication disorders. In Ball, M. J., Müller, N., & Spencer, L. (Eds.), *Handbook of Clinical Linguistics (2nd ed.)*, Hoboken: Wiley Blackwell, pp. 15–27.

Foppolo, F., Mazzaggio, G., Panzeri, F., & Surian, L. (2021). Scalar and ad-hoc pragmatic inferences in children: Guess which one is easier. *Journal of Child Language, 48*(2), 350–372. https://doi.org/10.1017/S030500092000032X.

Fox, A., Dishman, S., Valicek, M., Ratcliff, K., & Hilton, C. (2020). Effectiveness of social skills interventions incorporating peer interactions for children with attention deficit hyperactivity disorder: A systematic review. *The American Journal of Occupational Therapy, 74*(2), 7402180070p1-7402180070p19. https://doi.org/10.5014/ajot.2020.040212.

Freeman, R. D., Zinner, S. H., Mueller-Vahl, K. R. et al. (2009). Coprophenomena in Tourette syndrome. *Developmental Medicine & Child Neurology, 51*(3), 218–227. https://doi.org/10.1111/j.1469-8749.2008.03135.x.

Frith, M., Togher, L., Ferguson, A., Levick, W., & Docking, K. (2014). Assessment practices of speech-language pathologists for cognitive communication disorders following traumatic brain injury in adults: An international survey. *Brain Injury, 28*(13–14), 1657–1666. https://doi.org/10.3109/02699052.2014.947619.

Gabbatore, I, Guerrini, A. M. & Bosco, F. M. (2023). The fuzzy boundaries of the social (pragmatic) communication disorder (SPCD): Why is the picture still so confusing. *Heliyon, 9*(8), e19062. https://doi.org/10.1016/j.heliyon.2023.e19062.

Garraffa, M., Sorace, A., & Vender, M. (2023). *Bilingualism Matters: Language Learning Across the Lifespan*. Cambridge: Cambridge University Press. ISBN: 9781009333375.

Gaudreau, G., Monetta, L., Macoir, J. et al. (2013). Verbal irony comprehension in older adults with amnestic mild cognitive impairment. *Neuropsychology, 27*(6), 702–712. https://doi.org/10.1037/a0034655.

Gilliam, J. E., & Miller, L. (2006). *Pragmatic Language Skills Inventory*. Austin: Pro-Ed.

Goel, V., & Dolan, R. J. (2001). The functional anatomy of humor: Segregating cognitive and affective components. *Nature Neuroscience, 4*(3), 237–238. https://doi.org/10.1038/85076.

Gordon, A., & Zillmer, E. A. (1997). Integrating the MMPI and neuropsychology: A survey of NAN membership. *Archives of Clinical Neuropsychology, 12*(4), 325–326. https://doi.org/10.1093/arclin/12.4.325b.

Green, B. C., Johnson, K. A., & Bretherton, L. (2014). Pragmatic language difficulties in children with hyperactivity and attention problems: An integrated review. *International Journal of Language & Communication Disorders, 49*(1), 15–29. https://doi.org/10.1111/1460-6984.12056.

Greenberg, A., Bellana, B., & Bialystok, E. (2013). Perspective-taking ability in bilingual children: Extending advantages in executive control to spatial reasoning. *Cognitive Development, 28*(1), 41–50. https://doi.org/10.1016/j.cogdev.2012.10.002.

Grice, H. P. (1975). Logic and conversation. In Cole, P., & Morgan, J. (Eds.), *Syntax and Semantics* (Vol. 3). New York: Academic Press, pp. 41–58.

Halliday, M. A. K. (1975). Learning how to mean. In Lenneberg, E. H., & Lenneberg, E. (Eds.), *Foundations of Language Development*. New York: Academic Press, pp. 239–265. https://doi.org/10.1016/B978-0-12-443701-2.50025-1.

Hamed, S., Bradby, H., Ahlberg, B. M., & Thapar-Björkert, S. (2022). Racism in healthcare: A scoping review. *BMC Public Health*, *22*(1), 1–22. https://doi.org/10.1186/s12889-022-13122-y.

Hamilton, H., & Chou, W. Y. S. (2014). *The Routledge Handbook of Language and Health Communication*. London: Routledge.

Hansen, T. M., Qureshi, S., Gele, A. et al. (2023). Developmental disorders among Norwegian-born children with immigrant parents. *Child and Adolescent Psychiatry and Mental Health*, *17*(1), 1–11. https://doi.org/10.1186/s13034-022-00547-x.

Harris, M., & Pexman, P. M. (2003). Children's perceptions of the social functions of verbal irony. *Discourse Processes*, *36*(3), 147–165. https://doi.org/10.1207/S15326950DP3603_1.

Hauser, D. J., & Schwarz, N. (2020). The war on prevention II: Battle metaphors undermine cancer treatment and prevention and do not increase vigilance. *Health Communication*, *35*(13), 1698–1704. https://doi.org/10.1080/10410236.2019.1663465.

Hay, C. M., Sills, J. L., Shoemake, J. M. et al. (2024). F@# $ pain! A mini-review of the hypoalgesic effects of swearing. *Frontiers in Psychology*, *15*, 1–7. https://doi.org/10.3389/fpsyg.2024.1416041.

Hendricks, R. K., Demjén, Z., Semino, E., & Boroditsky, L. (2018). Emotional implications of metaphor: Consequences of metaphor framing for mindset about cancer. *Metaphor and Symbol*, *33*(4), 267–279. https://doi.org/10.1080/10926488.2018.1549835.

Henry, J. D., Phillips, L. H., Ruffman, T., & Bailey, P. E. (2013). A meta-analytic review of age differences in theory of mind. *Psychology and Aging*, *28*(3), 826–839. https://doi.org/10.1037/a0030677.

Hoffmann, A., Martens, M. A., Fox, R., Rabidoux, P., & Andridge, R. (2013). Pragmatic language assessment in Williams Syndrome: A comparison of the Test of Pragmatic Language – 2 and the Children's Communication Checklist – 2. *American Journal of Speech-Language Pathology*, *22*(2), 198–204. https://doi.org/10.1044/1058-0360(2012/11-0131).

Holler, J., & Levinson, S. C. (2019). Multimodal language processing in human communication. *Trends in Cognitive Sciences*, *23*(8), 639–652. https://doi.org/10.1016/j.tics.2019.05.006.

Howell, S., Varley, R., Sinnott, E. L., Pring, T., & Beeke, S. (2021). Measuring group social interactions following acquired brain injury: An inter-rater reliability evaluation. *Aphasiology*, *35*(11), 1505–1517. https://doi.org/10.1080/02687038.2020.1836315.

Iwashita, H., & Sohlberg, M. M. (2019). Measuring conversations after acquired brain injury in 30 minutes or less: A comparison of two pragmatic rating scales. *Brain Injury, 33*(9), 1219–1233. https://doi.org/10.1080/ 02699052.2019.1631487.

Kanner, L. (1943). Autistic disturbances of affective contact. *Nervous Child, 2* (3), 217–250. http://simonsfoundation.s3.amazonaws.com/share/071207- leo-kanner-autistic-affective-contact.pdf.

Kasher, A., Batori, G., Soroker, N., Graves, D., & Zaidel, E. (1999). Effects of right- and left-hemisphere damage on understanding conversational implicatures. *Brain and Language, 68*(3), 566–590. https://doi.org/10.1006/ brln.1999.2129.

Katerelos, A., Alexopoulos, P., Economou, P., Polychronopoulos, P., & Chroni, E. (2023). Cognitive function in amyotrophic lateral sclerosis: a cross-sectional and prospective pragmatic clinical study with review of the literature. *Neurological Sciences, 45*, 2075–2085. https://doi.org/10.1007/ s10072-023-07262-1.

Kecskes, I. (2014). *Intercultural Pragmatics*. Oxford: Oxford University Press.

Keegan, L. C., Hoepner, J. K., Togher, L., & Kennedy, M. (2023). Clinically applicable sociolinguistic assessment for cognitive-communication disorders. *American Journal of Speech-Language Pathology, 32*(2S), 966–976. https:// doi.org/10.1044/2022_AJSLP-22-00102.

Keegan, L. C., & Müller, N. (2022). The influence of context on identity construction after traumatic brain injury. *Journal of Interactional Research in Communication Disorders, 13*(2), 171–195. https://doi.org/10.1558/ jircd.21020.

Keegan, L. C., Müller, N., Ball, M. J., & Togher, L. (2022). Anger and aspirations: Linguistic analysis of identity after traumatic brain injury. *Neuropsychological Rehabilitation, 32*(8), 2029–2053. https://doi.org/10.1080/09602011 .2022.2071949.

Keegan, L. C., Suger, C., & Togher, L. (2021). Discourse analysis of humor after traumatic brain injury. *American Journal of Speech-Language Pathology, 30*(2S), 949–961. https://doi.org/10.1044/2020_AJSLP-20- 00059.

Keenan, T. R., & Quigley, K. (1999). Do young children use echoic information in their comprehension of sarcastic speech? A test of echoic mention theory. *British Journal of Developmental Psychology, 17*(1), 83–96. https://doi.org/ 10.1348/026151099165168.

Kidd, D. C., & Castano, E. (2013). Reading literary fiction improves theory of mind. *Science, 342*(6156), 377–380. https://doi.org/10.1126/science .1239918.

Kissine, M. (2021). Autism, constructionism, and nativism. *Language, 97*(3), e139–e160. https://doi.org/10.1353/lan.2021.0055.

Köder, F., Rummelhoff, C., & Garraffa, M. (2024a). Comparing pragmatic abilities across multiple languages in adults with ADHD. *Clinical Linguistics & Phonetics*, 1–16. https://doi.org/10.1080/02699206.2024.2374909.

Köder, F., Rummelhoff, C., & Garraffa, M. (2024b). Learning and using multiple languages: Experiences of adults with ADHD. *Ampersand, 13*, 1–9. https://doi.org/10.1016/j.amper.2024.100191.

Korrel, H., Mueller, K. L., Silk, T., Anderson, V., & Sciberras, E. (2017). Research Review: Language problems in children with Attention-Deficit Hyperactivity Disorder–a systematic meta-analytic review. *Journal of Child Psychology and Psychiatry, 58*(6), 640–654. https://doi.org/10.1111/jcpp.12688.

Lakoff, G., & Johnson, M. (1980). *Metaphors We Live By*. Chicago: University of Chicago.

Lampri, S., Peristeri, E., Marinis, T., & Andreou, M. (2024). Figurative language processing in autism spectrum disorders: A review. *Autism Research, 17*(4), 674–689. https://doi.org/10.1002/aur.3069.

Landau, S. F., Bendalak, J., Amitay, G., & Marcus, O. (2018). Factors related to negative feelings experienced by emergency department patients and accompanying persons: An Israeli study. *Israel Journal of Health Policy Research, 7*(1), 1–91. https://doi.org/10.1186/s13584-017-0200-1.

Leech, G. N. (1983). *Principles of Pragmatics*. London: Longman.

Lepper, G. (2009). The pragmatics of therapeutic interaction: An empirical study. *The International Journal of Psychoanalysis, 90*(5), 1075–1094. https://doi.org/10.1111/j.1745-8315.2009.00191.x.

Lethlean, J. B., & Murdoch, B. E. (1997). Performance of subjects with multiple sclerosis on tests of high-level language. *Aphasiology, 11*(1), 39–57. https://doi.org/10.1080/02687039708248454.

Littlemore, J. (2019). *Metaphors in the Mind*. Cambridge: Cambridge University Press.

Littlemore, J., & Turner, S. (2019). What can metaphor tell us about experiences of pregnancy loss and how are these experiences reflected in midwife practice? *Frontiers Communication*, 4, 1–17. https://doi.org/10.3389/fcomm.2019.00042.

Lorch, E. P., Diener, M. B., Sanchez, R. P. et al. (1999). The effects of story structure on the recall of stories in children with attention deficit hyperactivity disorder. *Journal of Educational Psychology, 91*(2), 273–283. https://doi.org/10.1037/0022-0663.91.2.273.

Lyddon, W. J., Clay, A. L., & Sparks, C. L. (2001). Metaphor and change in counseling. *Journal of Counseling & Development, 79*(3), 269–274. https://doi.org/10.1002/j.1556-6676.2001.tb01971.x.

Malkomsen, A., Røssberg, J. I., Dammen, T. et al. (2022). How therapists in cognitive behavioral and psychodynamic therapy reflect upon the use of metaphors in therapy: A qualitative study. *BMC Psychiatry, 22*(1), 1–12. https://doi.org/10.1186/s12888-022-04083-y.

Malvini Redden, S., Tracy, S. J., & Shafer, M. S. (2013). A metaphor analysis of recovering substance abusers' sensemaking of medication-assisted treatment. *Qualitative Health Research, 23*(7), 951–962. https://doi.org/10.1177/1049732313487802.

Manago, A. M., & McKenzie, J. (2022). Culture and digital media in adolescent development. In Nesi, J., Telzer, E. H., & Prinstein, M. J. (Eds.), *Handbook of Adolescent Digital Media Use and Mental Health*. Cambridge: Cambridge University Press, pp. 162–187.

Marini, A., Carlomagno, S., Caltagirone, C., & Nocentini, U. (2005). The role played by the right hemisphere in the organization of complex textual structures. *Brain and Language, 93*(1), 46–54. https://doi.org/10.1016/j.bandl.2004.08.002.

Marini, A., Spoletini, I., Rubino, I. A. et al. (2008). The language of schizophrenia: An analysis of micro and macrolinguistic abilities and their neuropsychological correlates. *Schizophrenia Research, 105*(1–3), 144–155. https://doi.org/10.1016/j.schres.2008.07.011.

Marocchini, E., Di Paola, S., Mazzaggio, G., & Domaneschi, F. (2022). Understanding indirect requests for information in high-functioning autism. *Cognitive Processing, 23*, 129–153. https://doi.org/10.1007/s10339-021-01056-z.

Mary, A., Slama, H., Mousty, P. et al. (2016). Executive and attentional contributions to Theory of Mind deficit in attention deficit/hyperactivity disorder (ADHD). *Child Neuropsychology, 22*(3), 345–365. https://doi.org/10.1080/09297049.2015.1012491.

Mashal, N., & Coblentz, S. (2014). Creative interpretations of novel conceptual combinations in aging. *Creativity Research Journal*, 26(2), 158–164. https://doi.org/10.1080/10400419.2014.901071.

Matthews, D. (2014). Introduction: An overview of research on pragmatic development. In Matthews, D. (Ed.), *Pragmatic Development in First Language Acquisition*, Amsterdam: John Benjamins, pp. 1–12. https://doi.org/10.1075/tilar.10.01mat.

Matthews, D., Lieven, E., & Tomasello, M. (2010). What's in a manner of speaking? Children's sensitivity to partner-specific referential precedents. *Developmental Psychology, 46*(4), 749–760. https://doi.org/10.1037/a0019657.

Mazzaggio, G., Foppolo, F., Job, R., & Surian, L. (2021). Ad-hoc and scalar implicatures in children with autism spectrum disorder. *Journal of Communication Disorders*, *90*, 106089. https://doi.org/10.1016/j.jcomdis.2021.106089.

Mazzaggio, G., Panizza, D., & Surian, L. (2021). On the interpretation of scalar implicatures in first and second language. *Journal of Pragmatics*, *171*, 62–75. https://doi.org/10.1016/j.pragma.2020.10.005.

Mazzaggio, G., & Shield, A. (2020). The production of pronouns and verb inflections by Italian children with ASD: A new dataset in a null subject language. *Journal of Autism and Developmental Disorders*, *50*, 1425–1433. https://doi.org/10.1007/s10803-019-04349-7.

Mazzaggio, G., & Surian, L. (2018). A diminished propensity to compute scalar implicatures is linked to autistic traits. *Acta Linguistica Academica*, *65*(4), 651–668. https://doi.org/10.1556/2062.2018.65.4.4.

Mazzaggio, G., Zappoli, A., & Mazzarella, D. (2023). Verbal irony and the implicitness of the echo: The processing of young and older adults. *Pragmatics & Cognition*, *30*(2), 412–443.

Mazzarella, D., & Pouscoulous, N. (2021). Pragmatics and epistemic vigilance: A developmental perspective. *Mind & Language*, *36*(3), 355–376. https://doi.org/10.1111/mila.12287.

Melo, F. S., Sardinha, A., Belo, D. et al. (2019). Project INSIDE: Towards autonomous semi-unstructured human–robot social interaction in autism therapy. *Artificial Intelligence in Medicine*, *96*, 198–216. https://doi.org/10.1016/j.artmed.2018.12.003.

Messer, R. H. (2015). Pragmatic language changes during normal aging: Implications for health care. *Healthy Aging & Clinical Care in the Elderly*, *7*, 1. https://doi.org/10.4137/hacce.s22981

Meulenbroek, P., & Cherney, L. R. (2021). Computer-based workplace communication training in persons with traumatic brain injury: The work-related communication program. *Journal of Communication Disorders*, *91*, 1–17. https://doi.org/10.1016/j.jcomdis.2021.106104.

Miranda-Casas, A., Ygual-Fernández, A., & Rosel-Remírez, J. (2004). Complejidad gramatical y mecanismos de cohesión en la pragmática comunicativa de los niños con trastorno por déficit de atención con hiperactividad. *Revista de Neurología*, *38*, 111–116. https://doi.org/10.33588/rn.38S1.2004058.

Mizuno, A., Liu, Y., Williams, D. L. et al. (2011). The neural basis of deictic shifting in linguistic perspective-taking in high-functioning autism. *Brain*, *134*(8), 2422–2435. https://doi.org/10.1093/brain/awr151.

Montemurro, S., Mondini, S., Signorini, M. et al. (2019). Pragmatic language disorder in Parkinson's Disease and the potential effect of cognitive reserve. *Frontiers in Psychology, 10*, 1–17. https://doi.org/10.3389/fpsyg.2019.01220.

Morales, J., Gómez-Ariza, C. J., & Bajo, M. T. (2013). Dual mechanisms of cognitive control in bilinguals and monolinguals. *Journal of Cognitive Psychology, 25*(5), 531–546. https://doi.org/10.1080/20445911.2013 .807812.

Murphy, D. R., Daneman, M., & Schneider, B. A. (2006). Why do older adults have difficulty following conversations? *Psychology and Aging, 21*(1), 49–61. https://doi.org/10.1037/0882-7974.21.1.49.

Naigles, L. R., Cheng, M., Rattanasone, N. X. et al. (2016). 'You're telling me!' The prevalence and predictors of pronoun reversals in children with autism spectrum disorders and typical development. *Research in Autism Spectrum Disorders, 27*, 11–20. https://doi.org/10.1016/j.rasd.2016.03.008.

Nippold, M. A., Uhden, L. D., & Schwarz, I. E. (1997). Proverb explanation through the lifespan: A developmental study of adolescents and adults. *Journal of Speech, Language, and Hearing Research, 40*(2), 245–253. https://doi.org/10.1044/jslhr.4002.245.

Noveck, I. A. (2001). When children are more logical than adults: Experimental investigations of scalar implicature. *Cognition, 78*(2), 165–188.

Noveck, I. (2018). *Experimental Pragmatics: The Making of a Cognitive Science*. Cambridge: Cambridge University Press. https://doi.org/10.1016/ S0010-0277(00)00114-1.

Noveck, I. A., & Sperber, D. (Eds.). (2004). *Experimental Pragmatics*. Basingstoke: Palgrave Macmillan.

O'Grady, S. (2023). An AI generated test of pragmatic competence and connected speech. *Language Teaching Research Quarterly, 37*, 188–203. https:// doi.org/10.32038/ltrq.2023.37.10.

OECD (2023). *PISA 2022 Results (Volume I): The State of Learning and Equity in Education*, PISA, OECD, Paris, https://doi.org/10.1787/53f23881-en.

Overcash, J. A. (2003). Narrative research: A review of methodology and relevance to clinical practice. *Critical Reviews in Oncology/Hematology, 48*(2), 179–184.

Panzeri, F., Mazzaggio, G., Giustolisi, B., Silleresi, S., & Surian, L. (2022). The atypical pattern of irony comprehension in autistic children. *Applied Psycholinguistics, 43*(4), 757–784. https://doi.org/10.1017/S0142716422 000091.

Papagno, C., Lucchelli, F., Muggia, S., & Rizzo, S. (2003). Idiom comprehension in Alzheimer's disease: The role of the central executive. *Brain, 126*, 2419–2430. https://doi.org/10.1093/brain/awg243.

Pardini, M., Gialloreti, L. E., Mascolo, M. et al. (2013). Isolated theory of mind deficits and risk for frontotemporal dementia: A longitudinal pilot study. *Journal of Neurology, Neurosurgery & Psychiatry, 84*(7), 818–821. https://doi.org/10.1136/jnnp-2012-303684.

Parola, A., Gabbatore, I., Bosco, F. M. et al. (2016). Assessment of pragmatic impairment in right hemisphere damage. *Journal of Neurolinguistics, 39,* 10–25. https://doi.org/10.1016/j.jneuroling.2015.12.003.

Parsons, L., Cordier, R., Munro, N., Joosten, A., & Speyer, R. (2017). A systematic review of pragmatic language interventions for children with autism spectrum disorder. *PloS ONE, 12*(4), 1–37. https://doi.org/10.1371/journal.pone.0172242.

Pell, M. D. (2006). Cerebral mechanisms for understanding emotional prosody in speech. *Brain and Language, 96*(2), 221–234. https://doi.org/10.1016/j.bandl.2005.04.007.

Pennebaker, J. W. (2000). Telling stories: The health benefits of narrative. *Literature and Medicine, 19*(1), 3–18. https://doi.org/10.1353/lm.2000.0011.

Petersen, R. C., Doody, R., Kurz, A. et al. (2001). Current concepts in mild cognitive impairment. *Archives of Neurology, 58*(12), 1985–1992. https://doi.org/10.1001/archneur.58.12.1985.

Petersen, R. C., Smith, G. E., Waring, S. C. et al . (1999). Mild cognitive impairment: Clinical characterization and outcome. *Archives of Neurology, 56*(3), 303–308. https://doi.org/10.1001/archneur.56.3.303.

Pexman, P. M., & Glenwright, M. (2007). How do typically developing children grasp the meaning of verbal irony? *Journal of Neurolinguistics, 20*(2), 178–196. https://doi.org/10.1016/j.jneuroling.2006.06.001.

Phillips, L. H., Allen, R., Bull, R. et al. (2015). Older adults have difficulty in decoding sarcasm. *Developmental Psychology, 51*(12), 1840–1852. https://doi.org/10.1037/dev0000063.

Phelps Terasaki, D., & Phelps-Gunn, T. (2007). *Test of Pragmatic Language, 2nd ed*. Austin: Pro-Ed.

Pijnacker, J., Hagoort, P., Buitelaar, J., Teunisse, J. P., & Geurts, B. (2009). Pragmatic inferences in high-functioning adults with autism and Asperger syndrome. *Journal of Autism and Developmental Disorders, 39,* 607–618. https://doi.org/10.1007/s10803-008-0661-8.

Pinker, S. (2007). *The Stuff of Thought: Language as a Window into Human Nature*. New York: Penguin.

Place, K. S., & Becker, J. A. (1991). The influence of pragmatic competence on the likeability of grade-school children. *Discourse Processes, 14*(2), 227–241. https://doi.org/10.1080/01638539109544783.

Plotas, P., Nanousi, V., Kantanis, A. et al. (2023). Speech deficits in multiple sclerosis: A narrative review of the existing literature. *European Journal of Medical Research, 28*(1), 1–12. https://doi.org/10.1186/s40001-023-01230-3.

Prado, J., Spotorno, N., Koun, E. et al. (2015). Neural interaction between logical reasoning and pragmatic processing in narrative discourse. *Journal of Cognitive Neuroscience,* 27(4), 692–704. https://doi.org/10.1162/jocn_a_00744.

Premack, D., & Woodruff, G. (1978). Does the chimpanzee have a theory of mind? *Behavioral and Brain Sciences, 1*(4), 515–526. https://doi.org/10.1017/S0140525X00076512.

Prideaux, G. D. (1991). Syntactic form and textual rhetoric: The cognitive basis for certain pragmatic principles. *Journal of Pragmatics, 16*(2), 113–129. https://doi.org/10.1016/0378-2166(91)90076-A.

Rapp, A. M., & Wild, B. (2011). Nonliteral language in Alzheimer dementia: A review. *Journal of the International Neuropsychological Society, 17*(2), 207–218. https://doi.org/10.1017/S1355617710001682.

Renauld, S., Mohamed-Saïd, L., & Macoir, J. (2016). Language disorders in multiple sclerosis: A systematic review. *Multiple Sclerosis and Related Disorders, 10*, 103–111. https://doi.org/10.1016/j.msard.2016.09.005.

Rietdijk, R., Power, E., Attard, M., Heard, R., & Togher, L. (2020). Improved conversation outcomes after social communication skills training for people with traumatic brain injury and their communication partners: A clinical trial investigating in-person and telehealth delivery. *Journal of Speech, Language, and Hearing Research, 63*(2), 615–632. https://doi.org/10.1044/2019_JSLHR-19-00076.

RoboKind. (2020). Robots4Autism. https://robots4autism.com/.

Rowe, M. L. (2000). Pointing and talk by low-income mothers and their 14-month-old children. *First Language, 20*(60), 305–330. https://doi.org/10.1177/014272370002006005.

Rowe, M. L., Özçalışkan, Ş., & Goldin-Meadow, S. (2008). Learning words by hand: Gesture's role in predicting vocabulary development. *First Language, 28*(2), 182–199. https://doi.org/10.1177/0142723707088310.

Sacco, K., Angeleri, R., Bosco, F. M. et al. (2008). Assessment battery for communication–ABaCo: A new instrument for the evaluation of pragmatic abilities. *Journal of Cognitive Science, 9*(2), 111–157. https://doi.org/10.17791/jcs.2008.9.2.111.

Salo, V. C., Rowe, M. L., & Reeb-Sutherland, B. C. (2018). Exploring infant gesture and joint attention as related constructs and as predictors of later language. *Infancy, 23*(3), 432–452. https://doi.org/10.1111/infa.12229.

Schaeffer, J., Abd El-Raziq, M., Castroviejo, E. et al. (2023). Language in autism: Domains, profiles and co-occurring conditions. *Journal of Neural Transmission, 130*(3), 433–457. https://doi.org/10.1007/s00702-023-02592-y.

Schmidt, M., Beck, D., Glaser, N., Schmidt, C., & Abdeen, F. (2019). Formative design and evaluation of an immersive learning intervention for adults with autism: Design and research implications. In Beck, D., Peña-Rios, A. Ogle, T. et al. (Eds.), *Immersive Learning Research Network. iLRN 2019.* Communications in Computer and Information Science, vol. 1044, Cham: Springer, pp. 71–85. https://doi.org/10.1007/978-3-030-23089-0_6.

Schouten, B. C., & Meeuwesen, L. (2006). Cultural differences in medical communication: A review of the literature. *Patient Education and Counseling, 64*(1–3), 21–34. https://doi.org/10.1016/j.pec.2005.11.014.

Searle, J. R. (1969). *Speech Acts: An Essay in the Philosophy of Language.* Cambridge: Cambridge University Press.

Semino, E. (2021). 'Not soldiers but fire-fighters' – Metaphors and covid-19. *Health Communication, 36*(1), 50–58. https://doi.org/10.1080/10410236 .2020.184498.

Semino, E., Demjén, Z., Demmen, J. et al. (2017). The online use of Violence and Journey metaphors by patients with cancer, as compared with health professionals: A mixed methods study. *BMJ supportive & Palliative Care, 7* (1), 60–66. https://doi.org/10.1136/bmjspcare-2014-000785.

Semino, E., Demjén, Z., Demmen, J. et al. (2017).The online use of violence and journey metaphors by patients with cancer, as compared with health professionals: A mixed methods study. *BMJ Support Palliat Care, 7,* 60–66.

Shinebourne, P., & Smith, J. A. (2010). The communicative power of metaphors: An analysis and interpretation of metaphors in accounts of the experience of addiction. *Psychology and Psychotherapy: Theory, Research and Practice, 83*(1), 59–73. https://doi.org/10.1348/147608309X468077.

Siegal, M., Surian, L., Matsuo, A. et al. (2010). Bilingualism accentuates children's conversational understanding. *PloS ONE, 5*(2), 1–8. https://doi .org/10.1371/journal.pone.0009004.

Siegal, M., & Varley, R. (2002). Neural systems involved in 'theory of mind'. *Nature Review, Neuroscience, 3*(6), 463–471. https://doi.org/10.1038/ nrn844.

Slabakova, R. (2010). Scalar implicatures in second language acquisition. *Lingua, 120*(10), 2444–2462. https://doi.org/10.1016/j.lingua.2009.06.005.

Sperber, D., & Wilson, D. (1981). Irony and the use-mention distinction. *Philosophy, 3,* 143–184.

Spina, M., Arndt, J., Landau, M. J., & Cameron, L. D. (2018). Enhancing health message framing with metaphor and cultural values: Impact on Latinas' cervical cancer screening. *Annals of Behavioral Medicine, 52*(2), 106–115. https://doi.org/10.1093/abm/kax009.

Spotorno, N., McMillan, C. T., Rascovsky, K. et al. (2015). Beyond words: Pragmatic inference in behavioral variant of frontotemporal degeneration. *Neuropsychologia, 75,* 556–564. https://doi.org/10.1016/j.neuropsychologia .2015.07.002.

Stapleton, K., & Fägersten, K. B. (2023). Swearing and interpersonal pragmatics. *Journal of Pragmatics, 218,* 147–152. https://doi.org/10.1016/j .pragma.2023.10.009.

Stephens, G., & Matthews, D. (2014). The communicative infant from 0–18 months: The social-cognitive foundations of pragmatic development. In Matthews, D. (Ed.), *Pragmatic Development in First Language Acquisition,* Amsterdam: John Benjamins, pp. 13–35. https://doi.org/10.1075/tilar .10.02ste.

Stephens, R., & Robertson, O. (2020). Swearing as a response to pain: Assessing hypoalgesic effects of novel 'swear' words. *Frontiers in Psychology, 11,* 1–10. https://doi.org/10.3389/fpsyg.2020.00723.

Sulpizio, S., Toti, M., Del Maschio, N. et al. (2019). Are you really cursing? Neural processing of taboo words in native and foreign language. *Brain and Language, 194,* 84–92. https://doi.org/10.1016/j.bandl.2019.05.003.

Surian, L., Baron-Cohen, S., & Van der Lely, H. (1996). Are children with autism deaf to Gricean maxims? *Cognitive Neuropsychiatry, 1*(1), 55–72. https://doi.org/10.1080/135468096396703.

Tager-Flusberg, H. (2000). Understanding the language and communicative impairments in autism. In Glidden, L. M. (Ed.), *International Review of Research on Mental Retardation. Special Issue on Autism.* New York: Academic Press, pp. 185–205. https://doi.org/10.1016/S0074-7750(00) 80011-7.

Taler, V., & Phillips, N. A. (2008). Language performance in Alzheimer's disease and mild cognitive impairment: A comparative review. *Journal of Clinical and Experimental Neuropsychology, 30*(5), 501–556. https://doi.org/ 10.1080/13803390701550128.

Thomas, J. (1983). Cross-cultural pragmatic failure. *Applied Linguistics, 4*(2), 91–112. https://doi.org/10.1093/applin/4.2.91.

Thurnherr, F. (2021). *Interpersonal Pragmatics and the Therapeutic Alliance: The Collaborative Work in Email Counseling.* Freiburg: NIHIN Studies.

Togher, L., McDonald, S., Tate, R., Rietdijk, R., & Power, E. (2016). The effectiveness of social communication partner training for adults with severe chronic TBI and their families using a measure of perceived communication ability. *NeuroRehabilitation*, *38*(3), 243–255. https://doi.org/10.3233/NRE-151316.

Togher, L., Power, E., Tate, R., McDonald, S., & Rietdijk, R. (2010). Measuring the social interactions of people with traumatic brain injury and their communication partners: The adapted Kagan scales. *Aphasiology*, *24*(6–8), 914–927. https://doi.org/10.1080/02687030903422478.

Togher, L., Wiseman-Hakes, C., Douglas, J. et al. (2014). INCOG recommendations for management of cognition following traumatic brain injury, part IV: Cognitive communication. *The Journal of Head Trauma Rehabilitation*, *29*(4), 353–368. https://doi.org/10.1097/HTR.0000000000000071.

Topol, E. J. (2023). Machines and empathy in medicine. *Lancet*, *402*(10411), 1411. https://doi.org/10.1016/S0140-6736(23)02292-4.

Väisänen, R., Loukusa, S., Moilanen, I., & Yliherva, A. (2014). Language and pragmatic profile in children with ADHD measured by Children's Communication Checklist 2nd edition. *Logopedics Phoniatrics Vocology*, *39*(4), 179–187. https://doi.org/10.3109/14015439.2013.784802.

Valian, V. (2015). Bilingualism and cognition. *Bilingualism: Language and Cognition*, *18*(1), 3–24. https://doi.org/10.1017/S1366728914000522.

Van Lancker, D., & Cummings, J. L. (1999). Expletives: Neurolinguistic and neurobehavioral perspectives on swearing. *Brain Research: Brain Research Reviews*, *31*(1), 83–104. https://doi.org/10.1016/s0165-0173(99)00060-0.

Vingerhoets, A. J., Bylsma, L. M., & De Vlam, C. (2013). Swearing: A biopsychosocial perspective. *Psihologijske teme*, *22*(2), 287–304. https://hrcak.srce.hr/108514.

Voss, C., Schwartz, J., Daniels, J. et al. (2019). Effect of wearable digital intervention for improving socialization in children with autism spectrum disorder: A randomized clinical trial. *JAMA pediatrics*, *173*(5), 446–454. https://doi.org/10.1001/jamapediatrics.2019.0285.

Vrticka, P., Black, J. M., & Reiss, A. L. (2013). The neural basis of humour processing. *Nature Review Neuroscience*, *14*(12), 860–868. https://doi.org/10.1038/nrn3566.

Washmuth, N. B., & Stephens, R. (2022). Frankly, we do give a damn: Improving patient outcomes with swearing. *Archives of Physiotherapy*, *12*(1), 1–4. https://doi.org/10.1186/s40945-022-00131-8.

Washmuth, N. B., Stephens, R., McAfee, B. et al. (2023). Using expletives to enhance therapeutic outcomes: A case report. *Health Psychology Research*, *11*, 89726. https://doi.org/10.52965/001c.89726.

Wellman, H. M., & Liu, D. (2004). Scaling of theory-of-mind tasks. *Child Development*, *75*(2), 523–541. https://doi.org/10.1111/j.1467-8624.2004.00691.x.

Wilson, D., & Sperber, D. (2012). Explaining irony. In *Meaning and Relevance*, Cambridge: Cambridge University Press, pp. 123–145. http://dx.doi.org/10.1017/CBO9781139028370.008.

Wimmer, H., & Perner, J. (1983). Beliefs about beliefs: Representation and constraining function of wrong beliefs in young children's understanding of deception. *Cognition*, *13*(1), 103–128. https://doi.org/10.1016/0010-0277(83)90004-5.

Winner, E., Brownell, H., Happé, F., Blum, A., & Pincus, D. (1998). Distinguishing lies from jokes: Theory of mind deficits and discourse interpretation in right hemisphere brain-damaged patients. *Brain and Language*, *62*(1), 89–106. https://doi.org/10.1006/brln.1997.1889.

Winner, E., & Gardner, H. (1977). The comprehension of metaphor in brain-damaged patients. *Brain*, *100*(4), 717–729. https://doi.org/10.1093/brain/100.4.717.

World Health Organization. (2001). *The World Health Report : 2001 : Mental Health : New Understanding, New Hope*. World Health Organization. https://iris.who.int/handle/10665/42390.

World Health Organization. (2007). *International Classification of Functioning, Disability, and Health*: *Children & Youth Version*: *ICF-CY*. World Health Organization.

Ying Sng, C., Carter, M., & Stephenson, J. (2018). A systematic review of the comparative pragmatic differences in conversational skills of individuals with autism. *Autism & Developmental Language Impairments*, *3*, 2396941518803806. https://doi.org/10.1177/239694151880380.

Yu, B. (2011). The emotional world of health online communities. In *Proceedings of the 2011 iConference (iConference '11)*. Association for Computing Machinery, New York, 806–807. https://doi.org/10.1145/1940761.1940914.

Acknowledgements

We would like to express our gratitude to the researchers in the language sciences community who are dedicated to building a bridge between linguistics – specifically pragmatics – and the clinical sciences. Linguistics is rarely central to the clinical agenda, and more evidence is needed to advocate for language assessments and therapies grounded in theoretical frameworks.

MG would like to acknowledge the *AttCom: the role of attention in the communication projects* team based at the University of Oslo (RCN project no. 315368) for the many proficuous discussions on pragmatics in clinical populations, and in particular Dr Franziska Köder, the PI of the project, for the opportunity to study in detail pragmatic profiles in adults with ADHD.

The authors want to thank Luca Bischetti for providing insightful comments on the first version of the manuscript.

Author Statement

Maria Garraffa and Greta Mazzaggio developed the structure of the Element, selected the materials, and revised the full manuscript in close collaboration.

Sections 1 and 5 are attributed to Maria Garraffa; Sections 2, 3, and 4 to Greta Mazzaggio.

9 781009 496025